THE PENALTY
KING

THE PENALTY
KING

THE AUTOBIOGRAPHY OF JOHNNY HUBBARD, RANGERS' STAR OF THE 1950s

BY JOHNNY HUBBARD
WITH DAVID MASON

FOREWORD BY SIR ALEX FERGUSON

First published by Pitch Publishing, 2015

Pitch Publishing
A2 Yeoman Gate
Yeoman Way
Durrington
BN13 3QZ
www.pitchpublishing.co.uk

A CIP catalogue record is available for this book
from the British Library.

ISBN 978-1-78531-079-9

Typesetting and origination by Pitch Publishing

Printed by TJ International, Cornwall, UK

Contents

Dedication and Thanks from Johnny Hubbard

To the big umpire in the sky who delivered me into one great country and then another, while blessed with skills that allowed me to fulfil my dreams. Above all, he gave me a family to be proud of, with a beautiful wife, kids and grandchildren.

I also dedicate it to football fans everywhere and especially those of the greatest club there is – The Rangers.

Finally, I would like to thank my great friend David (Mason) for his patience and support. I cannot thank him enough for helping me to bring my story to print.

Acknowledgements

WHILST many have helped to contribute to the delivery of this story about a very special man, particular thanks are due to Jeff Holmes, Paul Camillin and Jane Camillin for helping to bring the publication to fruition, John Beckett for the first proof-reading, John Gilligan for being a good friend to Johnny, Colin Shearer for assisting in the promotion, Rangers Football Club and finally Craig Brown, Martin Ferguson and Alex Ferguson for their uniquely personal memories of the little man's wonderful career.

Foreword by
Sir Alex Ferguson
CBE

WHEN I was asked several years ago about the best goal I had ever seen, I had no hesitation in plumping for one scored by Johnny Hubbard against Celtic on New Year's Day, probably around 1955. I can still see it now – a corner for Celtic, who were shooting into the Broomloan Road end, was cleared out to the left-hand side, where little Johnny Hubbard was lurking midway in his own half. Bobby Evans, the stalwart Celtic midfield player, was closing him down as he received the ball. In a flash, Johnny danced past him and the excitement grew at the Rangers end as he flew forward, attacking the Celtic centre-half Alex Boden, whom he beat, then he went past Frank Meechan, the little left-back. It left him one-on-one with Celtic's goalkeeper Bell, whom Johnny also went past with relative ease, to leave him with a tap-in. The game ended 4-1 to Rangers with Johnny Hubbard scoring a hat-trick, but the highlight was that goal.

It is a pleasure to be asked to write this foreword for Johnny's autobiography, as the Rangers fans of that era will agree that his contribution to the club's history was huge. In a time when wingers hugged the touchline, Johnny was the typecast of that generation. Seldom did wingers stray from that position and it was the inside-forwards and wing-halves whose job it was to service them. It was a period when Rangers FC had a strong link with South Africa and Norman Arnison and Don Kichenbrand were prominent players at Ibrox around the same time as Johnny. It must have been a massive decision to leave his home country, but courage was something that Johnny didn't lack, as all fans will remember. Full-backs were not shrinking violets!

Of course, I cannot write this piece without referring to his prowess in taking penalty kicks where he was a master and he went two years without failure until he missed against Airdrie at Broomfield. Their goalkeeper Walker was the man who went down in the history books as stopping Johnny's run. I was at that game and was stunned that he missed a penalty and like all the other Rangers fans couldn't believe it, however, his total of 60 goals from penalty kicks with only three missed was some going.

Having joined Rangers in 1949, he spent ten years at Ibrox, playing in 300 games and scoring 129 goals, which for a winger is quite exceptional and adding to his amazing record, he was the first South African to play and score in the European Cup. In 1959, he joined Bury and stayed there for three years before finishing his career at Ayr United. After retirement as a player he became a PE teacher and youth development coach as there was no way the grass was going to grow under his feet. His energy has never waned and every time I meet him, I am struck by his sheer personality. He still travels almost every week to see his beloved Rangers, with the same enthusiasm as if he was still a player. 'Remarkable' is about the only way I can describe that love of life. This is not just a story of 'once upon a time there was a footballer'. This is a journey of a young man from Pretoria in South Africa, eager to do well and prepared to succeed in a foreign country.

Well done Johnny Hubbard!

Sir Alex Ferguson CBE

Preface by David Mason (Rangers Football Club)

WHEN I joined The Rangers Football Club as club historian in 1986, the name Johnny Hubbard was already familiar to me. He was revered as one in a line of great wingers at Ibrox Park who despite his lack of physical stature, built a career that rightly placed him among the giants of the game. South African born and bred, he had been lured to Rangers and to Scotland in 1949, when he was just 18 years old. At that time, he was little more than a youngster with potential, but he eventually broke through to become an important component in the last great side that the legendary Rangers boss, Bill Struth assembled. He was to remain with the Light Blues for a decade, during which time he played 300 games and scored 129 goals. Indeed, he also became something of a legend through his prowess from the penalty spot. During his time with

Rangers he successfully converted 60 penalty kicks into goals from 63 attempts, earning the title 'The Penalty King'. Few disputed that he truly was the master of all from the spot. However, over the next few years I would learn that there was much more to Hubbard.

Here was a man who moved from continent to continent, swapping the bright blue African skies for the grey smog of Glasgow, simply to play the game he loved. The lure was professional football and although he knew little of Rangers before he arrived at Renfrew Airport, he could receive no better introduction to the club than in his first meeting with the man he still respectfully calls 'Mr Struth'.

The manager was to become something of a fatherly figure to the young South African, and figures strongly in his story. Struth was a strict disciplinarian, who it was often said ruled his charges with an iron fist inside a velvet glove. In Hubbard's case, Struth never had to enforce any discipline or instil professionalism. Hubbard already had a focus that he had carried with him to Scotland – one that was borne of a determination to succeed.

Nearing the end of his own career, Struth nurtured Hubbard's along until ill health took its toll and Scot Symon took the managerial reins at Rangers. The transition of managers should have been seamless. Symon, a former player was, himself, one of Struth's boys and appeared of a similar mould.

For Hubbard, however, the change was not welcome and even though many years have passed since he pulled on the Rangers jersey for the last time, he remains embittered. His reflections prove an insight into life at

Rangers in the last years of the great Bill Struth and the contrasts of the 'new era' under Symon.

By the time I had been honoured with the opportunity to preside over the club's archives, Hubbard's playing days had long passed. After ten years at Ibrox he moved on to Bury Football Club, before he returned to Scotland with Ayr United. It was a move that would take him to a new home in Prestwick, where he still lives.

I was a young child when he finally hung up his boots but I did once get the chance to see him on the playing field. Then, as one of the younger players in a Rangers v Celtic 'Old Crocks' match at Adamslie Park, Kirkintilloch, he showed more than a little skill in torturing the ageing Celtic defenders that day. Indeed, they knew him well – he still retains the enviable record of being the only foreign player to have scored a hat-trick for Rangers against their Old Firm rivals. That match in Kirkintilloch may have been meaningless to all but the charity that benefitted from the large gate money. To me, however, this was a chance to see some Rangers greats and if the Light Blues were the stars that day, there were none brighter than Hubbard.

When Johnny finally retired from the game in 1964, he did not turn his back on the game, or on sport in general. Inspired to give something back, he turned to community service, almost single-handedly at times, revitalising local interest in a variety of sports, including tennis, swimming, cricket and, of course, football. For many years he cajoled the public authorities, local businessmen and former colleagues to support his enthusiasm in bringing coaching and facilities to the benefit of literally thousands of youngsters. 'If it hadn't been for you

Mr Hubbard, my life may have turned out differently,' one youngster confessed and there have been countless similar accounts. It is typical of the widespread respect that still exists within the Ayrshire community for the impact that this little South African has had on the lives of local youngsters. He was awarded an MBE in 1998 in recognition of his enormous contribution to the community and was honoured with the chance to carry the Queen's Baton through the Ayrshire town that he now calls home.

Today, he maintains his ties and affection with Rangers, attending almost every home game, even though he has to endure the discomfort and inconvenience of public transport. However, he feels at home with the fans and they still love him. So much so, that they made him an Honorary Member of the Rangers Supporters' Trust in 2007. The club's own tribute to him followed in 2008, when he was elected into the Rangers Hall of Fame. Johnny Hubbard's life is a wonderful story and there is no better way to learn of it than through his own words. It is a story 'out of Africa', which began in Pretoria back in 1930.

Prologue

The rule which instigated the penalty kick was instituted by the four nations of the International Football Association Board at Glasgow's Alexandra Hotel on 2 June 1891. They agreed that:

If a player intentionally trip or hold an opposing player, or deliberately handle the ball within 12 yards from his own goal line, the referee shall, on appeal, award the opposing side a penalty kick, taken from any point 12 yards from the goal line under the following conditions—all players, with the exception of the player taking the penalty kick and the opposing goalkeeper, who shall not advance more than six yards from the goal line, shall stand at least six yards behind ball; the ball shall be in play when the kick taken; a goal may be scored from the penalty kick.

I AM John Gaulton Hubbard, or to the followers of that great football team they call 'The Rangers' and team-mates from a bygone era, I am plain and simple, 'Hubbie'! It's a name that perhaps lacks a little imagination, certainly in comparison to the likes of

'Tiger' Shaw, 'Corky' Young and 'Big Ben' Woodburn, all of whom I played alongside through a glorious spell in the 1950s. However, while I am 'Hubbie' to most, I have another nickname. Indeed, when I decided to commit my life story to print, it was the late great Sandy Jardine, a Rangers star of the 1960s through to the 80s, who immediately ventured the title of this book. He said – it must be called 'The Penalty King'.

I doubt whether Sandy ever saw me even take a penalty, but he was aware of my reputation as the player who rarely missed a spot-kick. Indeed, I only missed on three occasions, although I don't regard these as 'misses'. They were saved by the goalkeeper! However, if the keepers had success on these occasions, there were 60 other penalties where they could do little more than pick the ball out of the net.

It was not the only thing I did in the game, of course, and I look back with some pride on a career that blossomed with Rangers over a ten-year spell at the famous Ibrox Park. It was a career that introduced me to some wonderful players and one of the greatest football managers the game has seen – Bill Struth. Under his guiding hand, I was set on a course that would establish me in one of the best teams he created, tasting the champagne of success with domestic trophies. It was a career that also took me to representative honours with both Scotland and South Africa!

It is easy to see, therefore, why I hold my time at the club with such affection. You see, at Rangers, I lived the dream – one that I had harboured through my adolescent years until I arrived in Scotland from South Africa in 1949. My dream was to become a professional football player and although I had talent and earned a contract at Ibrox, I was to learn that there was more to Rangers than simply football. Under Struth, I was to learn that this club, that I had barely heard of before I arrived, was an institution. It was a club where great standards were expected of those honoured with the chance to play in their royal blue jersey. A club where only the best was considered good enough and where the foundations of my adult life would be built. These ten years at Ibrox were the happiest of my life.

It did not all end there, of course, and my life has been a very happy one, with a wonderful family including wife Ella, three great children and eight lovely grandkids. I enjoyed playing football with other clubs and then, when my career ended, giving something back to both sport, and to society. Little did I imagine that this would culminate in Her Majesty Queen Elizabeth awarding me an Honorary MBE for services to the community. However, I do not believe I would have achieved anything in my career without the experience of my formative years in my homeland of South Africa. It is there, therefore, that my story starts.

1

My African Childhood

MY name is John Gaulton Hubbard and I was born in Pretoria on 16 December 1930 – a beautiful South African city far removed from the one that I would ultimately call home. Situated in a fertile valley surrounded by hills, it was known as 'Jacaranda City' after the trees which dominated the suburbs, adding a splash of colour with their beautiful and characteristic blossom.

I can still remember how they scented the warm moist summer air and even the dry cool breezes of winter. My memories often take me back there and to the many happy times I spent under the African skies. It was a place which was so different from Scotland, where I would eventually settle and live with great contentment, but it is a city where part of me remains. My memories are of a very pleasant place to live with a diverse culture rooted in the city's tribal past and later Afrikaans influences.

Unlike Glasgow, whose history dates back many centuries, Pretoria was a relatively modern place in comparison. The city was established in 1855 by the 'Boers' – farmers of Dutch origin who had migrated from the Cape colonies and it had become the administrative capital of South Africa. But around the turn of the 19th century, it had also been at the heart of the conflict which became known as the Boer War. Following the great Zulu wars, Britain had tightened its imperial control on the Transvaal region in the late 1870s, but they faced great resistance from the city fathers – the Voortrekkers[1] – who were not ready to relinquish governance of the town they had founded. They rebelled against the British forces in a fierce, but short conflict in 1880. This First Boer War, as it became known, did not bring stability and a second war followed nine years later. This time the war lasted three long years and, although Britain succeeded and maintained overall control, the governance of the country remained within Transvaal. In 1910, it led to the formation of the Union of South Africa. When peace was returned to the old Transvaal, there was tranquillity, but the city retained a vibrancy and sense of adventure, reviving the spirit of the old Voortrekkers.

I mention this, not simply to give some background to the history of my country, but because my roots can be firmly traced to the Second Boer War. I often reflect that if it had not been for the conflict, I would not be here! If Pretoria was characterised by its diversity, with its native Africans and Afrikaans dominating, my background

---

1 The Afrikaans word for 'pioneers'.

was also somewhat cosmopolitan. While both of my parents were South African – my father Raymond from Pretoria and my mother, Johanna, from Port Elizabeth in the south – their families had come from opposite ends of the world. My father was from Australian stock, while my mother was half-Irish.

Her father – my maternal grandfather – came to Africa with the British expeditionary forces to fight in the Second Boer War, presumably around 1889. Many Irish people joined the army at that time to escape the poverty within their own country. When the conflict was over, they were faced with the prospect of returning to the desperation of Ireland. Like many, my grandfather deserted. He was not alone, because many of the soldiers in the Irish regiments followed suit. Besides, fundamentally, they did not support the action of what they saw as the imperialist army suppressing the settlers.

It was not all about the politics of the situation or the poverty of home, however. There were many other attractions to life under the African sun. The country had a much more agreeable climate than the often cold and wet Ireland and prospects for employment in the new country looked much more promising in the aftermath of the war. Maybe my grandfather even had romantic interests, because he soon got married to the woman who was to become my grandmother. By then, he was destined never to leave South Africa and he managed to get work in the building trade. It eventually led to a job in the construction of the first bridge over the Orange River. I do not know much more about him at that time, but it was a little bit of the folklore of the family that he was involved in such a prestigious bridge.

The bridge was probably funded by Britain because, following the war, the country had offered the Boers money for reconstruction. Most of that money was used to improve the infrastructure of the country, including the railway and that is where my father's family come in to the story. The great drive towards reconstruction in the post-war era provided many jobs for the African people, but it also encouraged immigration for those looking for a land of opportunity. While the Boer War brought my mother's father to the country as a soldier, my father's family were lured to South Africa by opportunities that arose in the country in the aftermath – particularly in the railway. One of the most important projects that followed the war was the construction of a new railway station in Pretoria, which was built in 1910. It served as a terminal for a number of railway lines coming from places like the Cape and Natal, however, the station was not constructed using British money. The Transvaal government had funded the project with their residual cash rather than surrender the money to the new South African government at the time of reunification. It was a case of use it or lose it.

My grandfather had been a railway worker in Melbourne and he saw the opportunity to work in the new railway network in South Africa. He managed to get fixed up in a job as a stationmaster in Pretoria and he and my grandmother settled in the city. Sometime later my father was born and I suppose it was natural that when he grew up, he would also find his career directed towards the railway. He duly continued this family tradition by becoming an inspector of locomotives oils – a good job that was to eventually take him all over the world. It was possibly through one of these trips that he was to meet a lovely lady from Port Elizabeth – my mother! They were clearly taken with each other and romance seemed to have blossomed, because they soon got married and set up home in Pretoria, amid the blooming jacaranda.

Mom and dad began to build their family shortly after they were married with Ruth the first born, followed by Dorothy, Daisy, Raymond and finally me, the youngest. I loved every one of my siblings and I was close to each of them. I loved them not just as any brother would his brothers and sisters, but because they were genuinely very nice people. Being the baby of the family, I found that they were all very keen to play a part in my upbringing and I loved them for that too. It was wonderful being the youngest and I loved being the baby! They would spend time taking me out for trips around Pretoria and at home they would entertain me. I was never left wanting as they tended to all my needs and I reflect that, as a youngster, I could not have wished for better siblings.

I have such happy memories of them all at home, but as I grew older and became increasingly more inde-pendent, the family began to naturally fragment as the older members moved on. Ruth and Dorothy married and were the first to leave home when I was just a youngster, so I spent less time with them, but I shared some of my happiest times with Daisy and Raymond. Ordinarily you might think that I would have had the greatest affinity with my brother, but I actually had much more in common with Daisy. Raymond was essentially a 'bookworm' and more academic, but Daisy was the one who shared my passion for sport and tennis in particular. Raymond was not disinterested in sport and we would often play tennis together, but when he came on to the court with me, his interest in winning quickly evaporated as I hit winning shots past him! That generally sparked off a new game where he would try to hit me with the balls. Regardless of the individual interests of my brothers and sisters, we had one common bond – we were family.

There was another member of the family that I should not forget to mention – a small dog named 'Hitler'. To many people, that might have seemed a strange name for us to choose, but the Fuhrer was in the news at the time as he continued his march across Europe. We just thought it seemed suitable for our snappy little dog, but it did not turn out to be a good omen for him. One day he ran out of the house, strayed under a car and was killed. I ran around to see mom at the tennis club, with tears streaming down my face. I was yelling in despair, 'Hitler's dead. Hitler's dead!' I did not draw much in the way of sympathy from the club members and there were plenty long and puzzled looks as she put her arm around me. Later I found out that the people at the tennis club had wondered why I was in tears because Hitler had died!

The family home was a nice three-bedroomed bungalow in Tulleken Street, on the southern side of Pretoria. The family had moved in to it shortly before I was born. It was very close to the railway line and the main station, but was in a nice suburban part of town. The street was in a quiet area and the people who lived there were a reflection of the cosmopolitan population of the city, with families from many backgrounds, all living happily together. There were lots of children in the street and, although I would play with and have fun with my brothers and sisters, I had no shortage of friends.

Unlike kids in Scotland who have little time to play outside after school in the winter, we had the benefit of the climate and the geography of South Africa combining to make it a great place to grow up as a child. There was not much of a twilight so school times were adjusted to the light. In the summer we would go to school at 7.55am and finish at 12.55pm and in the winter everything moved forward by 30 minutes. This left plenty time to play long into the afternoon and as soon as I came home I would always go outside to play. By 5pm it was generally dark, or about to get dark and I headed home for dinner with the family, eagerly awaiting another day out in the sunshine playing with my friends.

As a child, playing with my friends in Tulleken Street would almost always involve games with a ball. We would play cricket, football, tennis and many other games, using the street as our playing ground. I really did not have time for anything else as all I wanted to do was to go out to play. Even today I still get regular flashbacks of these happy days when garden gates would be goalposts or a tree would become a wicket. If we did not play in the street, we would usually head over to Berea Park and the Railway Institute playing fields, which were situated a short distance away from our house. It was there that my love affair with sport was to truly blossom.

These fields, which were transformed from a cattle compound into fine sports grounds, were the first to be created in Pretoria and opened in 1882. I also heard that it was the first place that a motor car was displayed to the public in South Africa. For me, however, the playing fields were heaven. The facilities that Berea Park offered were wonderful with 12 tennis courts, two football fields, one rugby pitch, a baseball pitch and three big bowling greens. The facilities were certainly in marked contrast to what was available in Scotland at the time, particularly in the great cities. While we had a multitude of sports we could play in South Africa, it seemed that in Scotland, sport was dominated mainly by football, or to a much lesser extent rugby. There is no doubt that weather was a detrimental factor in Scotland, of course, but the facilities at the Railway Institute's grounds were all-year and every aspiring sportsman's dream.

In the summer months, all of the playing fields were cleared for cricket and the ground was the venue for some first-class matches, featuring the North-Eastern Transvaal Cricket Union and then later, the Northerns Cricket Club. Cricket was one of the more popular games among South African children and one of the kids in our group, Kenny Funston, went on to play in 18 Test matches for South Africa. His son also went on to become a first-class cricketer. South African kids at the time tended to play many sports and, like many of us, Kenny's excellence in sport was not confined to cricket. He gained soccer colours for North-Eastern Transvaal and hockey colours for Orange Free State. That was fairly typical at the time. South Africa was very sports orientated and there were opportunities to play most of the popular field sports.

Life in my early years was not all about sport of course and when I had reached six years of age, I went to the English-speaking Hamilton Primary School. I was to become good at Arithmetic and History, and I excelled at Afrikaans, but, unlike my brother Raymond, I was not academic. As the day at school dragged on, I could not wait to set my books aside to go outside and into the sunshine with a ball to enjoy the clean, fresh air. Even in these early years of my school life, I had already decided I wanted to become a professional sportsman. Mom was very supportive of my enthusiasm for sport, but she was also keen on the arts and encouraged me to develop other talents and interests. When I was eight, for example, she considered that I had a fine soprano voice and sent me for singing lessons. It did seem to nurture some hidden talents and that year I won certificates for mime, recitation and singing, but after six months I decided that the arts were not for me. I was a pretty active child and I always wanted to be outside playing, so being stuck inside in music classes did not really sit well with me.

Although I had a lot of other interests at the time, my life really revolved around my passion for sports. This was to be a feature of my life from my earliest years. As the months passed, I spent more and more of my time at Berea Park, cycling there as quickly as I could after school each day. During the summer, we played cricket and in the winter when the pitches had been restored, we played mainly football (or soccer as we called it), rugby, or occasionally hockey.

In this environment with opportunities to play almost anything, it was not difficult to get involved and reach a decent standard in every sport. By the time I had reached ten, I was already active in a number of different sports, but my love for the game of football, in particular, was growing.

As my siblings grew up and turned their interests elsewhere, the sports grounds at Berea Park were to become increasingly important to me. At every opportunity I looked to get involved in a game of football and if I could not play because there was a match, I would spectate. These matches would tend to involve my local side, Berea Park, who played at the grounds every other Saturday. They were more than just a team to me, however. I believed that they were a famous soccer club and, although they were nowhere near the standing of the British clubs at the time, they were a good side. Some measure of their standing is that England manager Roy Hodgson had his first experience of coaching at Berea Park in 1973. During his time there he played for Berea and coached the first team, as well as the under-14s and some of the schoolkids. It obviously gave him an introduction to football coaching, although not a successful one – he took them to relegation.

Although I had heard of some of the British football teams, especially those that toured the country, the game in South Africa revolved around the local and regional teams and Berea Park was my team. I loved them as much as any young Rangers fan adores his club today and, just as the Light Blues supporters have their idols, I had my favourite too. My hero was a Scot named 'Snowy' Walker – one of Berea Park's star players. When I went to watch the team, I would always stand next to the entrance to the dressing room and when Snowy came out to take to the field, he would stop, break his Black Jack chewing gum into two pieces and give me one of them. I was in awe of this man whom I saw as a real football star. He was my inspiration and at half-time after we had watched the first 45 minutes, I could not wait to play soccer with a tennis ball along with all of the boys. We would play out every move, taking on the mantle of our heroes. I was the leader of the pack, honing my skills on that little ball and dreaming of the day when I could emulate Snowy.

Snowy Walker was every bit the hero figure and his sporting skills went beyond the football field. Like many great sportsmen, he had good eye-to-ball co-ordination and when he retired from playing football, he took up bowling, reaching the top in that sport too. In fact, he reached greater heights in bowls than he did in football. He won the South African singles championship a number of times and he was also a member of the 'fours' that won the team championships on several occasions. His standing in the game was such that he went on to represent South Africa at the Empire Games and his team won the gold medal in 1950. Even today he is considered to have been one of the best bowlers that South Africa has ever produced. He was such a big star in the country that they later named a street after him in Pretoria.

When I eventually left South Africa several years later, I never imagined that I would ever meet Snowy Walker again, or that if I did, I doubted if he would ever remember me. However, in 1956, long after I had become established at Rangers, he turned up at the front door of Tynecastle Park, completely out of the blue. We had just played against Hearts in a Scottish Cup match and he had taken in the game. I was deeply honoured that he had remembered the little boy who waited faithfully by the dressing room doors of Berea Park almost 15 years earlier. He told me that he had followed the progress of my career in South Africa, then on to Scotland when I went to Rangers. Meeting him once again was such a wonderful surprise and from that day on he was to remain a family friend. Even after he died some time later, my wife and I remained friends with his wife and daughter.

There is no doubt that as a youngster, I gained a lot of my inspiration and desire to become a professional sportsman from watching Snowy perform on the pitch. I suppose that this ambition to be like him was one of the reasons that I was never really interested in school. If Hamilton Primary was not going to be a focus for academic interest, however, it did at least give me my first competitive game at the age of 11 – in rugby, not football. Rugby was not my favourite, or best, sport and my team-mates were not cut out for it either. Quite simply, we were not very good. Our greatest 'success' in a series of uninspiring performances was a 33-0 defeat! To their credit, the schoolmasters recognised that perhaps we would do better if we changed codes to soccer – probably because all of the kids were deflated. It was a welcome solution all round and, since I had some experience of playing the game, they made me team captain. I played inside-right and at last I had found something in school that now held some interest for me.

The decision by the school to give up on rugby and let us play football was inspired. We turned out to be a far better football team than rugby side, which was not difficult, and we made good progress. By now, the daily lessons of school were becoming a mere sideshow as my focus and attention switched firmly to football. Once, we were due to play a cup game, which was arranged to be played at the end of the day when the classes were over. As I sat in the geography class that morning, I was cleaning my boots under the table in preparation for the game. The teacher spotted me and I was hauled out of the class and sent along to see the principal, Mr du Plessis. When he was told of my misdemeanour, he was not a happy man. He told me that I would not make a living from playing football and that schoolwork was much more important to my future. Unrepentant, I told him that one day I would be a professional soccer player, but that show of self-confidence did not seem to impress him at all. He said, 'Today you are getting the cane and that's that!'

With corporal punishment prevalent in schools at that time, I was duly given the cane and a stern lecture. Certainly the punishment worked because I never again cleaned my boots in class. However, it did not alter my view on where my future lay, or my lack of interest in regular schoolwork. Ironically, the school's motto at that time was 'Ipsum Nosce', which translates 'Know Thyself'. Perhaps if Mr du Plessis had taken heed of that, he may have realised that I knew more about me than he did. Maybe that is why he eventually changed the motto to 'For Others'. In hindsight, I think he realised the futility in punishing me, as he knew that I had more interest in sport than the academic part of school. I am sure he knew that no amount of scolding would change my outlook, but it went further than that. It was not simply about my lack of interest in school and an over-enthusiasm for sport. I wanted sport to play a major part in my life and I reckoned that the 'big umpire in the sky' had given me a talent. I was determined I was going to make full use of it and I was convinced that I would become a professional footballer. Moreover, I was determined that not even Mr du Plessis's cane could change that.

I loved playing football and it was becoming more and more of a respite from some unhappy times at home – but only when my father was there. Although I had a wonderful life as a youngster in the Transvaal, our family setting was hardly idyllic. The railway took my father away from home for long periods, but, ironically, these were the times when our home was happiest. When he was at home, he was strict with all of us and the atmosphere in the house was strained. I remember on one occasion he caught me swearing and dragged me into the bathroom where he forced me to eat a bar of soap. It was a stupid thing to do and it nearly killed me. I survived, of course, but, importantly, this unsavoury incident had a marked effect on our relationship.

To me, this was not the kind of behaviour that would create the kind of bond a son would want with his father. In fact, I had no bond with him at all. His relationship with my mother also deteriorated and we later learned that he was a bit of a philanderer. They ultimately divorced when I was around 12 and he left our family to live in Durban with another woman, who had a few children of her own. He never had any more children and when he walked out, he left his only family behind, leaving my mom to raise us. We never saw him again. It must have been enormously difficult and stressful for my mom, especially as things became very tight financially.

He had left her with no money or any other means to bring the family up. The whole situation was very upsetting for the family, but the experience probably bonded the rest of us closer together.

If my father was a huge disappointment, my mother Johanna was an angel and she was to be the rock upon which our family was built. She had seen her husband leave and shortly afterwards her daughters had grown up, got married and also left. She must have felt that her family was disintegrating when her husband left, but she held everything together for us. However, despite having what must have been a very low income, we never at any time felt that we were poor. We always seemed to manage to get by and, apart from my father's absence, we were a happy and contented family.

Looking back on these days I realise the huge sacrifices that mom must have made to give us such a great life. She must have given up so much to keep us clothed and fed. We certainly had enough fruit in the house from the trees in the garden – two peach, a pear and a few quince. However, I can never recall any time when we did not have other foods on the table. Neither was I ever conscious of our family life being anything other than normal, even if it was without a father in later years. Whenever I needed new clothes or sports equipment, they were always there for me. Mom would buy me tennis shoes, sports boots and even my own cricket bat. She would also always show interest in what I was doing, coming to watch me play football and tennis, or to take me to the cinema to watch the kids' films on Saturday mornings. When we were together at home, we would play ludo or cards. She put everything into the family well-being and no one could have wished for a better mother.

When all of my sisters and my brother eventually moved out and got married, I lived alone in the house with my mom for six years. The house remained a happy one, although I was not around so often. By then, this love of sport had completely taken over my life and I would spend most of my time at the Berea Park playing fields. Mom never remarried, although she enjoyed the company and friendship of an older man who lived nearby. They would go to Berea Park for a drink occasionally and we often wondered why she did not remarry, but she seemed happy for things to remain that way.

In my later years in South Africa, before I went to Scotland, there was just mom and me. However, in the first 12 years of my life, there was another woman in my life. She was introduced to us in circumstances which reflected the political and cultural situation of South Africa, but might seem quite alien to those born and bred in the United Kingdom. At the time, the white man ruled the country and a policy of separatism prevailed. It was a system that would eventually cast a shadow over life in the country.

2

Separatism And Apartheid

IF my mom was the most important woman in my life at that time, there was another who played a key part in my upbringing up to my teenage years – a black girl called Martha. This brings me to one of the most controversial aspects of life in South Africa at the time – apartheid – the Afrikaans word for 'separateness'. Pretoria was the 'capital of apartheid' to many people in the wider world, but I have to say I did not experience it as it was perceived and indeed, it was not even a word I was familiar with. There *was* separatism, where the cultures of the blacks and the whites were distinct and remained apart, but not generally with any formality. It was seen in South Africa as a natural division of people from vastly different cultures and if it was a system, I was raised within it and never knew anything else. As a youngster, I did not see any difficulty with people of whatever race living in their own ways and in their own communities – especially when they were so different. Indeed, there was little dissension among the black people.

At that time there was a relatively even split in the population between whites and blacks living in and around the city. The communities were certainly segregated, but I never saw it as the strict apartheid that the world came to know and loathe. The blacks lived mostly in the townships outside the town, but they often lived quite close to the whites in the town centres. The separatism resulted in us having our own schools while the black people had theirs. We all travelled on the same buses, with the blacks sitting at the back, while the whites would take the seats at the front. When it came to public facilities and entertainments, however, there were definite restrictions on the blacks. They could not attend cinemas, which were designated 'white-only' or swim in the local swimming pool. They *could* come and watch football matches and other sports events, but they had their own standing areas. Even for those who played soccer, there were white leagues and black ones. I am not condoning this way of life or advocating the system of segregation that I experienced then, but it was all that I knew as a youngster in South Africa.

Living in such an environment, I was always aware of the huge cultural differences that existed between us and the blacks, but they were none more noticeable than when the workers at Berea Park gathered to eat after work. While we would eat sandwiches and fruit, the black workers would devour their own food – mielie-meal. This was a coarse flour mix made from maize which was cooked in a large pot. It would then be dumped on to a clay plate for them to tuck in to with their fingers, as cutlery was quite alien to them. I did not see anything wrong in this habit at dinner or with the food they would eat, but it was quite different from my own meals. These were just some of the obvious cultural differences, which I found very interesting at times. However, the differences were not just in the food they ate. When they gathered, there would often be a bit of a commotion. Occasionally I would go to a hilltop at Marabastad to watch them congregate and then batter each other.

Marabastad was a culturally diverse community near the centre of Pretoria and from the hill I could look down on the black boys playing football or fighting. Their football matches were quite normal, but when they faced up to each other to fight, the conflicts were quite savage and apparently ritualistic, with blood flowing freely. I never ever dared venture down from the hill to where they gathered, but I found their antics fascinating, although quite different from what would be expected in the white communities.

There will be some who will perhaps venture that gang fights were commonplace at one time in Glasgow, too and I suppose football hooliganism is rooted in the same tribal antics that lead to conflicts. However, in Marabastad, these bloody clashes seemed to be something of a routine, though not one that I ever wanted to get too close to.

To anyone who did not live in South Africa or had not experienced life there at that time, this separatism must have seemed quite deplorable. However, it was quite normal to me and it was not until I left the country that

I realised that I had been raised in a quite unusual society. I am often asked about apartheid in South Africa, but for me it was simply the way of life with different peoples. The whites and the blacks had different cultures and we stayed within our own respective communities. Most of the black people knew that the white man was not there to dominate them and I never sensed any ill-feeling with the majority. We just got on with our lives in our own ways and there was a general harmony in the society. The blacks would live off the work created by the whites and they would often do the jobs that white people tended to avoid.

If the system worked in the time I was there, the separatism became more strident in 1948 just before I left the country, when it became real 'apartheid'. This coincided with a change in the political system when the main Afrikaner parties based their campaign on the policy of apartheid. They won and immediately introduced laws that institutionalised racial segregation which then became much more ingrained in the system. By then, blacks over the age of 18 had to carry identity cards and employment became restricted as 'white-only' jobs began to emerge.

There was also a prohibition on marriage between blacks and whites. Although black people had generally lived in their own areas through choice prior to 1948, the election *compelled* them to live in out-of-town areas – the townships, dedicated to their specific tribe. What had existed through preference among the races prior to 1948 developed into this policy of racial segregation and was quite different from the separatism that existed in the South Africa I knew. It was a segregation with degradation, which did not exist in my time in the country.

The stigma of colour did not only impinge on the rights of the black Africans. Two of my friends were treated as 'black' in the community because of their skin colouration, even though one, Nikola Molonis, was actually Greek. He was a great football player and I did try to engineer the chance for him to come to Scotland, but it did not work out. Another of my friends who was a great footballer, Eddie Latouf, came from North Africa, and was also treated as 'black'. They were very much part of our group and we also built up a good relationship with a big black lad, Ruben Bennett, at Berea Park. He was employed to look after the boots and the balls at the playing fields and we would meet him every day. Although he was not part of our community, it made no difference to how we treated him. We knew lots of nice black people, but there were also unruly elements who gave their community a bad name, thieving and murdering. This impacted on how they were perceived by the white community and this is perhaps where the roots of apartheid lay. There were also militant elements, but the vast majority of black people seemed to be content and prepared to live under white governance at that time.

I was brought up to respect everyone, regardless of their colour or culture. My family did not have any black friends and certainly none would be expected to come to our home, but it was not through any dislike for black people. Having lived in both South Africa and the United Kingdom I can look back on the system of segregation that I experienced from a more balanced viewpoint than others who did not. For me, it was a way of life and there did not seem to be any problems in our society, with both blacks and whites living within their own cultures. However, when the South African government institutionalised apartheid, the outside world took notice, particularly through sport.

The system gained notoriety in a famous clash between the cricket boards of South Africa and England in 1968. The situation arose when the England cricket team proposed to tour South Africa and included within their side a non-white player, a South African immigrant named Basil D'Oliveira. At the time, South African cricket was strictly all white, with no black players in their leagues and certainly none in the national side. The South Africans objected and cancelled the tour, causing some consternation and uproar around the globe. It cast a shadow over the country which was then branded racist by the world community.

It was completely wrong to ban D'Oliveira of course, but I could understand why the government took the decision they did in preventing the tour from taking place. When I played cricket it was a game exclusively for whites and I suspect that the government of South Africa was concerned that if it allowed D'Oliveira to tour, many blacks would then seek to play in the cricket clubs in South Africa. It would have weakened the apartheid system upon which the whole governance was based and may have increased militancy among the black population. The country was not ready for that upheaval, or that kind of decision, although ultimately there would be no holding back of the tide of opposition from other countries and within South Africa itself.

The reaction over D'Oliveira brought the contrast between the countries sharply into focus for me. In Britain there were hardly any black people at that time, or at least it seemed that way in Glasgow. In Pretoria, prior to 1948 we had a system that managed different cultures, in a manner that seemed normal to me, but that was obviously out of step with life in the UK. What was the normality in South Africa was alien everywhere else it seemed. My feelings were unchanged because I saw it as a system based on cultural changes, not disrespect. Indeed, the divisions in society seemed deeper in Scotland when I arrived. While most people in South Africa were Protestant, there were some Catholics, but I was never conscious of religion being an issue until I came to Scotland. Religious bigotry was thriving in Glasgow which was not something I was familiar with in South Africa. However, it appeared to be an acceptable part of the culture in a diversity which, in some ways, mirrored the separatism in my homeland. Even today Catholic and Protestant children go to different schools.

Although I was raised in a system of segregation, I was raised to respect black people, so when I arrived in Glasgow, I treated people alike, whether Catholic or Protestant. I think it becomes a question of personal values and I was brought up to respect everyone. By giving that respect, I have also received it from others. It is a good way to live. Rangers have always been regarded as the Protestant club in Glasgow, while Celtic are supported mainly by Catholics. Nowadays, I have lots of banter with Celtic fans and I like to think that I show everyone the same level of respect. It was not a fair system in South Africa, but I was brought up in a culture where respect was paramount and this is something I brought with me to Scotland.

Regrettably, the subsequent isolation of South Africa from world sport denied many great sportsmen of the chance to compete around the globe. This is the luck of the draw and the way of life for sportsmen who often have to contend with the impact of politics in which they have no control. You have to play with the cards you are dealt just as D'Oliveira did in moving from his homeland to continue to develop his career outside the country. South Africa had changed from the country I left and the D'Oliveira incident brought things sharply into focus for many people. By then it had become castigated for its racism, but for me, South Africa was once a country of harmony and that was how I remembered it. I did not know Basil D'Oliveira, but as a keen cricketer and a South African, I would have liked to have had a chat with him to reflect on these days of great upheaval and his role in bringing about the changes that would ultimately take place.

Although the white and black communities did not mix socially, they were reliant upon each other. The blacks would seek employment within the white communities, where many jobs were created. The blacks would often undertake the type of work that whites resisted, such as cleaning the streets. It was also common for many black women to come looking to help care for white children, as nannies. So, when I was born, a black woman arrived at our house one day seeking to be the nanny to the new baby. Her name was Martha. My mother employed her, but when she took on the role, she stated that she would leave when I reached 12 years of age. I do not know why that particular age was a milestone in her plans, but that was the timescale she put on her time in looking after me. Martha called me 'Boss Johnny' and from then on, she stayed with us, living in a 'kaya' – a special room in the back garden, where she had her own facilities. She became an important part of our family and my closest friend through that period, completely dedicated to caring for me.

Throughout those early years of my life Martha was always by my side, walking me to and from school every day. She would often take me to the cinema on Friday evenings and since she was not allowed to enter, she would wait outside for the film to finish, before taking me home. Separatism prevented her getting in to the swimming pool too, but it did not hinder her from taking me there, where she would wait until it was time for me to leave. At Berea Park, she would also watch me play football from the 'black-only' area of the stadium. Martha was my companion and protector and it seemed that there was nothing she would not do to ensure that I suffered no harm.

I recall one occasion when I was stung by a bee in the garden. It had come out of a hollow wood pipe frame used for the grapevine, where there were a few bees nesting. In the commotion, Martha realised that the bees were disturbed and could swarm out to attack us. Without hesitation, she stuck her finger in the hole of the pipe to prevent any more coming out, even although it was inevitable that she would be stung by some very angry bees. However, she wanted to protect me and it is a measure of both her courage and commitment that she did this to save me from further distress.

The bees certainly presented some danger to me on that occasion but Pretoria was a pretty safe place to live with regards to the wildlife in the community, so she did not have to fight off wild animals to protect me! Africa conjures up images of great beasts roaming the bushveld or the savannah. The wilds certainly have more exotic animals than commonly found on Glasgow Green, but inner-city Pretoria was a little different. Although we were deep in the African continent, I did not see a lot of the animals you might imagine. I had pen-friends in Germany and I used to joke with them that I had a lion in my garden, but the only time I actually saw such wildlife was in the town's zoo.

There were not many animals wandering the suburbs of Pretoria, but I did have a couple of encounters that scared the wits out of me. Once I went around to the back garden to dispose of some rubbish in the bin. As I was just about to drop it in I saw a big black snake curled up at the bottom. I did not hang around and dropped the rubbish before running back in terror into the house. On another occasion, I was swimming with some friends in the Apies River, which flowed alongside Berea Park. I saw a stick floating on the water and reached across to grab it. As I took hold of it I realised that it wasn't a stick at all, but a water snake. I threw it away as quickly as I had picked it up, then got out of the river faster than you can imagine.

Away from these live animal encounters and sport, most of my excitement came from the cinema. I enjoyed going to the movies, either with Martha on a Friday evening, or with mom on a Saturday morning. Westerns were all the rage in those days and John Wayne was everyone's hero. I also remember seeing *Gone With the Wind*, which is a long movie and it played well into the night. At the end of the film, I remember that the cinema played 'God Save the King', since the people were still very patriotic and mindful that the country was a British protectorate. However, not everyone was happy to stand while the national anthem played. It was quite common for the Afrikaners who were still disaffected by the British control, to leave as soon as the national anthem began. We always stood to attention when it played.

I have a lot of pleasant memories of Martha and our days out – especially one when she took my brother Raymond, my sister Daisy and me to Pretoria Zoo in the one pram. Raymond was perched at the front, Daisy was on the back and I was snuggled inside. They were happy days and Martha was very much part of our lives and family at that time. However, when I reached the age of 12, she announced that she would leave, just as she had always promised when she first came into our employ. We did not want her to go and she did not want to leave, but she had made a commitment that she would not break and simply moved on. It was a very sad day for us all when she left, simply saying 'goodbye' as she walked out the door, down the path and out of our lives. Sadly, I never saw Martha again, but I will always remember her friendship and companionship.

I suppose I had reached the stage where I no longer needed a nanny, but she had become more than that to us all through these 12 years. I had begun to mature and my eyes had become firmly fixed on a life in sport, but Martha left a huge gap in our lives. I often wonder what became of her, if she ever married and had children of her own. If she did, they could not have had a better mother, because she was a wonderful companion to me and an enormous part of my life in those early years.

A few years ago I made a rather nostalgic trip back to Pretoria and to Tulleken Street. Although the city has seen many changes in recent years, the street remains almost as it did when I was a child, although our house has gone, replaced by flats. However, the palm tree which was in our garden remained – along with the memories of many happy days in the sunshine which were so vivid. Many of my happy memories reflect the big part that Martha played in my early life, for which I am eternally grateful.

3

A Good Little 'Un

THERE is a saying often used in sport, 'A good big 'un is better than a good little 'un', but if it was a popular myth believed by many, I was always determined to show that it did not apply in my case. I was always smaller than my contemporaries so I knew that I would have to work a bit harder to show that I was at least as good as any player that I came up against. It became my motivation in every sport I took part in as I strove to get fitter, faster and be more skilful than the big 'un. In football, I always worked hard at physical training and I practised with a ball at every opportunity to improve my football ability. Through the philosophy that fitness and ability more than compensated for my small stature, I had no problem in fitting in even among the older boys.

On one occasion, I found that my stature earned me a nickname that I did not understand until sometime later. After school lessons I used to head off to Berea

Park for a lunchtime game with about 100 black boys who worked on the Railway Institute's grounds and tea bars. As I mentioned, despite the separatism that existed in South Africa at the time, I had no problem in joining the black boys for a game. However, there was a distinction between me and the other boys that went beyond colour. It was not just that I was the only white boy, but I was the only player with boots. They welcomed me into their game and I was always given lots of encouragement by them. To them, I was not Johnny Hubbard, but they christened me 'Johnnie Walker' and it was a name that would stay with me all the time I played football in South Africa.

I did not really understand the significance of it at the time, until I eventually went to Glasgow. One day I saw a Johnnie Walker whisky bottle with the famous character strutting proudly across the label. It was then that I realised that the black boys back in South Africa probably considered me as small as the wee man on the bottle!

By the time I was 12, I had already been a regular playing football around Berea Park and I must have caught the eye of the club officials. They approached to invite me to play for the under-16 team. I had never played for a team outside of school, so I was humbled that they thought me good enough. It was a significant stage in my development. I settled in very quickly and realised that not only was I much younger than the rest of the players in the team, but I was also much smaller. I still have the team picture from that year, which shows me sitting proudly in the front row, but noticeably smaller than the other boys.

Despite being very small in comparison, I could quite easily pitch myself in with the bigger boys. I was not intimidated by the prospect of playing with, and against boys who were considerably bigger at all, because I held this firm belief that fitness and ability were all that mattered. Since I had worked at both of these attributes, I had an inherent confidence that I could comfortably settle into the team – and I did so without any trouble. Fitting in at that under-16s level was some confirmation to me that I was making good progress with the game.

Playing for what could be called a proper team encouraged me to improve my game further. At every opportunity I would go to Berea Park, to work away for hours with the ball, dribbling, playing keepie-uppie, passing and shooting. I knew that to be a better player I would need to be two-footed and my left was my weaker foot. For a whole week I worked on it until I was as comfortable on my left as I was on my right. This may sound like a particularly short time in which to build up confidence and ability with my weaker foot, but I could adapt very well, left or right. I could be ambidextrous and although my right side was naturally the stronger, I did not have much difficulty playing with the left hand or foot. When it came to tennis and badminton I was a right-hander, and I also bowled right-handed at cricket. However, on the cricket pitch, I was a left-handed bat.

This brings me to the penalty kick. I had always struck the ball well when shooting or passing and whenever I played with my friends, I would take penalties. When I joined the under-16s at Berea Park, I got the chance in one game to take a spot-kick. I cannot remember too much about it, other than that I scored. I must have done so convincingly because from that day I was the regular penalty taker for the team. I could not have imagined that this would start me on a road that would eventually see me crowned 'The Penalty King'. That day at Berea Park, I struck the penalty as I have always done – I hit the ball low and hard to the corner with my right foot, but more of that later.

By now, football was my favoured sport and I was spending increasing amounts of time on playing the game with friends or the under-16s, quite apart from the long hours in training. However, I had not given up on other sports and when I found time away from the football, I played many others such as cricket and tennis, reaching a good level of ability in most that I took part in. I even became a good swimmer, probably to ensure that I could swim quickly away from water snakes!

Although Berea Park gave me access to most of these sports, school offered a good opportunity to play other games too. I had left Hamilton Primary School and by the time I reached 14, I had moved to Pretoria Boys' High School, which was, and still is, one of the biggest and most respected in South Africa. At that time there were 600 students, of which 90 per cent were boarders, but I was among the remaining ten per cent of day students, travelling back and forward each day from Tulleken Street. By then, the blackboard held no interest for me, but the school was impressive and it opened up the door to more opportunities in a whole range of sports. While many saw the school as a place where kids could further learning and academia, pushing towards a successful career, for me it was simply another outlet for activities on the playing field.

The first week at the school gave the kids a chance to get to know their way around this great establishment as well as what it offered in recreation. I found that there were several sports that you could take part in and I was keen to participate in every one they offered. When they held the cricket trials I watched as they quickly whittled down the numbers, organising all the participants into eight teams. It seemed that they had initially selected the teams based upon their expectations on the ability of the kids. Those of good build and height that they considered had the potential to excel as cricketers, were selected for team one and the next batch went into team two, etc. By the time they had reached team eight, the only kids left were those that did not look at all sporty. There was more than a hint of Darwin in this process, although not exactly of natural selection. If there was some expression of the 'survival of the fittest', the school was at the heart of it.

In the trial, team one played team two, three played four and I was chosen in team five to play against team six. They probably did not expect much from me, but I was quite handy with a bat, because we had always played at Berea Park or on the road at Tulleken Street. I eased into the game without any fluster and quickly made my mark with fifty runs and five wickets. By the following week, I was instantly promoted into the first team. Again, the team photograph shows a rather diminutive Johnny Hubbard among the bigger boys. My size was no handicap and I held my own in the team.

One of the highlights of the school year in that first term was the sports day and, as you might imagine, I was at the heart of it. I raced in the mile and finished second behind a chap called Crozier. He clocked four minutes 23 seconds, which was not a bad time for a 19-year-old, but at five years younger, I was very happy with my time of four minutes 58 seconds. Then there was the cross-country when I took part in a field of over 300 and ended up winning the event by 20 yards from another 19-year-old.

Away from the track and field I also sought out competition on the tennis court. I had already become a decent tennis player having played at the local club, and had some agility from dodging balls hit by Raymond! I had heard of the Northern Transvaal School tennis competition so I seized the chance to enter and added my name to the list of competitors for the junior (under-16) and senior (under-19) levels. I fought my way through to the final of the under-16s, where I beat a boy called J. Fourie 6-2, 6-4. I also battled through to the final of the under-19s competition, where I defeated his older brother by two sets to one; 2-6, 6-0, 8-6. These successes brought me my first trophies and I still have the two small cups at home. My eldest son Raymond maintains that they are now so old that they are only held together by dirt!

I enjoyed playing tennis and I maintained a long, but sadly unfulfilled ambition to play at Wimbledon. Perhaps if I had devoted as much time to the game as I did to football, I could have fulfilled that desire but tennis was never anything more than a sport to me. Football was where I really saw my future as a professional. The games in the Northern Transvaal School competition had shown once again, however, that my stature did not limit my ability to compete with older and bigger boys. Indeed, perhaps it may have been disarming to my competitors when they saw me take to the court – and eventually capture the titles.

Through the next two years I played with various school teams and continued at Berea Park, where I was becoming stronger and more confident. Football dominated all of my available time, but I still enjoyed cricket and when I was 16, I had started to play for a side called Iscor, which was in the Third Division of the Pretoria District Cricket Association league. The match reports were carried by the *Pretoria News* and I got some good coverage when I reached 129 not out against Pretoria. The newspaper covered many of our matches and with an average of 39 runs through the season, I was frequently mentioned in the press. I meticulously removed these newspaper cutting, adding them to my increasing scrapbook.

If I was beginning to catch the eye with the bat, I was also gaining some credibility as a good all-round sportsman. The school was aware of this and they encouraged me to join other teams and particularly the rugby side, but I turned them down in preference to football. Others would try to draw me into their teams and I loved competition, whether it was cricket, tennis or on the athletics field, but no matter the progress and headlines I was making in other sports, I had already made up my mind where my future would lie. Football was now my life and everything I did was planned with the intent that I would eventually become a professional footballer.

At 16, and after two years, I had come to the end of the road with a school that had given me a great chance to develop my interests and ability as a sportsman, but offered me little else. I had lost interest in schoolwork long before then and I had made up my mind to leave at the first opportunity. I suppose my mother was reconciled to that a long time before and everyone agreed that leaving school was for the best. In the summer of 1947, I walked out of the Pretoria High School gates for the last time and realised that now life would be different. The opportunity to play sports at the school had gone and, most importantly, I realised that now I would have to earn some money.

I had lost touch with my father, but his association with the railway did manage to open up an opportunity of work which I followed up. They gave me an office job and as the latest member of the Hubbard family to work with the railway company, I continued something of a tradition, but I simply hated it. After just two months I could not tolerate being confined to the office anymore and I managed to get fixed up with an apprenticeship as an electrician. It was better than being deskbound, but that work did not stimulate me either. I lasted just three months when I saw a vacancy in a sports shop. They were looking for a shop assistant and the work was much closer to my passion. It was also the first chance I had to earn an income through sport, although perhaps not quite in a way that I had envisaged! The role was ideal, however and, at last, I could get some direction in my life, but I still retained my deep desire to become a professional sportsman, not a sports retailer.

With school behind me, I reached a fine balance in my life between work to earn some income and time to concentrate even more on my sports. It seemed that everything was starting to fall into place and after having played four years for the Berea Park under-16 team I was now ineligible. However, the natural progression for those good enough would be a place in the senior side and I had already attracted the attention of the selectors. Berea Park played in the regional league system that operated in South Africa at the time and they were one of the top sides around. From the days of Snowy Walker, I had been a big supporter of the team and I was thrilled when I was asked to sign up for them. Shortly after joining them, I was selected to play in my first senior game – a Transvaal League match against their fierce rivals, Municipals. Even although I was just 16, I had played in many games, but that first match for the senior side at Berea Park was different. I saw it as the start of my football career proper, and the significance of the game to me is highlighted by the scrapbook of newspaper cuttings which I retain to this day. On the first page I wrote:

> John Hubbard
> Saturday 24 May 1947 vs Municipals at Berea Park
> Won 2-1
> Age   16 yrs 3 mths
> Height   5ft 2ins
> Weight   116 pounds
> Position   Wing

I clearly felt that this was the start of a long career and I wanted to mark the significance of that first big match. If it was a milestone of a day for me, however, there were some who were unhappy with my selection, believing that I was too young for the side. But, if I was a good little 'un, the selectors clearly also felt that I was a good young one. My performance in what turned out to be the ideal debut, silenced the doubters as the team won comfortably. I did not feel at all overawed as I settled into the game, playing on a pitch I knew well. The match was covered by all of the local newspapers and their praise for my performance was fulsome and humbling.

A report in the *Pretoria News* talked of my tender years and highlighted the pre-match criticism from some quarters that my selection had attracted. However, it commented that any such disquiet had been well and truly quelled by my performance, especially considering my direct opponent. I played on the left-wing against right full-back Tom Bornman, who was 6ft 3in and a South African international player. As I mentioned, I believed that there was nothing to fear against the bigger player if you were fitter and faster – and I was.

The *Sunday Times* in Pretoria reported that I 'delighted the crowd with some very clever play despite the attentions of Bornman'. The correspondent for the *Sunday Express* wrote, 'Hubbard, not 5ft in height, proved a thorn to the Municipals defenders.' The *Sports Express* wrote, 'One of the outstanding players was Berea Park's wing, Hubbard.'

The plaudits for my performance that day against Municipals did not only come from the press corps. A few days after the game I received a nice letter from one fan, a Mr W.G. Taylor, who congratulated me on my performance. He wrote that I had 'a magnificent game' and that my goal had followed a 'beautiful ingenious move'. Importantly, he had said that he felt I would reach the top of the ladder. These were great words of encouragement and I stuck the letter into my scrapbook and have it to this day.

My performance that day sealed my place in the team for good and I started to fill out my scrapbook with newspaper cuttings reporting my performances. One newspaper, *The Star*, reported that I 'certainly knew what to do with the ball', but with a growing discontent in the game over the lack of talent coming through, it also took the opportunity to have a go at the South African FA. It lamented that the authorities were not far-sighted enough to import professional coaches to bring out the latent talent in young South African players to fulfil their potential and become internationals. Maybe it was right, because I never received proper coaching, but it did not concern me. I felt that I was making good progress in the game on my own and earning some recognition on the way. If I continued to get such reviews, I knew that my time would come. I just had to keep doing what I enjoyed most – playing football and then we would see where that would take me.

Three weeks after my debut, Northern Transvaal were due to play a professional team from Scotland – Clyde FC. The Transvaal team was selected from the best players in the province and was the next level up in standard for players from the regional league teams like Berea Park. Despite my impressive start and my performance against Bornman, I was not picked for the regional side. The selectors felt that I was both too young and too small and that my entry into the league had come too late to allow me to be considered. After all, I had just played a few games at the top level and they must have been concerned about my inexperience. This concern was also raised by the *Pretoria News* which commented, 'Hubbard must have been a strong candidate for inclusion in the team in the eyes of some, but his extreme youth and lack of big game experience were against him.'

It had been a whirlwind start to my senior career and, if there was a little disappointment that I did not make the Northern Transvaal side, I knew that my time would come sooner or later.

The opportunity to stake a claim for a place in the regional side came around much quicker than I expected. Despite being left out of the big match, I was selected to play in the regional under-16s team which faced Southern Transvaal in the curtain-raiser before the match. The manager of Clyde, Paddy Travers, watched the match and remarked that he was 'very impressed with Hubbard' before adding, 'I will invite him over to Scotland in a couple of years' time when he grows and puts on a few pounds.'

Travers was a respected football manager in Scotland and he had already taken Clyde to a Scottish Cup win before the tour of South Africa. I was honoured and excited by the interest he had shown in me. If I needed any more inspiration, these comments helped and it was just another sign that I was moving in the right direction and catching the eyes of those who could perhaps make my dream of professional football come true.

Although I was beginning to make my mark in football both locally and regionally, I did not abandon my interest or participation in other sports. I played for the FP's hockey team and also Northern Transvaal, but

I was also attracting some attention at the wicket. One newspaper, the *Sunday Express,* talked of the 'exceptional promise' that I showed as a cricketer, saying that I was 'probably the most promising all-rounder in Pretoria'. I enjoyed cricket and to many, it must have seemed that this was where my sporting future could lie. I scored a century in my second game for Pretoria's second team and was immediately promoted to the first team. I was then selected to play against Johannesburg and I went on to score 68 runs, which was not bad for a 16-year-old. The performance was all the more satisfying since the top South African international leg-spin bowler Denis Begbie was among their bowlers.

Apart from hockey, football and cricket, the *Sunday Express* also highlighted that I was excelling in athletics and had also reached a good level in tennis. Indeed, at the Berea Park Tennis Club, I won the singles and then went on to win the mixed doubles, partnered by my mom. Mom was a good partner and played club tennis until she was 65. She also played a high standard of bowls. I imagine that this is not the normal trend of such things, with boys generally taking their sporting abilities and interests from their father, not mother. In fact, my dad was not sporty at all. However, my mom was very good at sports and I reckoned that I must have inherited that enthusiasm and aptitude for the ball from her.

Although it was very pleasant to succeed at other sports, I was not distracted from my ambition to make the grade in football. Indeed, I was positively encouraged with the way my career was progressing. I had made a great start with Berea Park and, although I missed out on the game against Clyde, within a few months

I had come to the attention of the Northern Transvaal regional selectors once again. They picked me to play in a trial match ahead of an important Currie Cup tie with Western Province in Cape Town. The match was played on my home ground at Berea Park in front of a big crowd and, being a local lad, the spectators were keen to see me play well. I did not disappoint them as I had a good game and felt comfortable with the way I played. I felt that I had done more than enough to warrant a place in the team and the Northern Transvaal team selectors agreed – I was in.

Just as playing for the Berea Park senior side marked an important stage in my development as a player, my debut for the regional side was also hugely significant. Despite the great pressure burdened on me, given my age and height, I did not let the selectors down. We played well and the side went on to win 3-1. Once again the press plaudits were generous in their praise of my performance. The *Pretoria News* ventured that I had 'no equal as a wing in the province at the moment'. *The Star* reported, 'Some Pretoria enthusiasts were predicting bigger things for him [me] within the next two or three seasons.' Even the *Cape Times* reported that I had a 'fine game'.

Throughout it had been my burning desire to become a professional footballer, but I was realistic about my career progression and my age. I knew that at just 16, I would have a few more years of development before I could step up to the professional ranks – especially since that would involve a move away from South Africa. It was in the background to this that I had to turn down my first opportunity to become a professional, which came just after the Currie Cup match had ended. As I was ready to leave the ground, I was approached by a scout from Huddersfield Town, in England. He had been in the crowd and he told me that he wanted me to turn professional and join the Yorkshire side. It was great to receive such a compliment that I could do something for his team and in many ways, it was humbling. However, I had to turn it down – I knew that I was still too young at that time. I was confident that another opportunity would arise, but at that moment, the time was not right.

4

Who's That Team They Call 'The Rangers'

AFTER I joined the senior side at Berea Park, the games were coming thick and fast as I then also became established in the regional Transvaal side. After one match for Northern Transvaal, when we beat our Eastern neighbours by six goals to two, *The Mail* reported that I showed 'rich promise … with the ability to hit the ball with either foot and beat his man both ways'.

Huddersfield Town had already declared an interest but I was also attracting the attention of other English clubs and the paper reported that I was 'oozing football from every pore', and, 'Arsenal, the English champions, have been advised that here is a boy worth thinking about.'

I was obviously aware of the growing interest around me and although the press reviews were encouraging, I kept my feet firmly on the ground. I continued to work away at my game, determined to improve and be ready when the time was right. Around this time, Alex Prior, a former Hibernian and Scotland full-back, was coaching in South Africa and had taken up duties at Berea Park. He asked me if I was interested in playing football in Scotland, but, just as I had turned down the Huddersfield scout, I still felt that I was too young to consider a move away from home. I politely turned down this interest from Mr Prior, but somehow I knew that it would not go away. The press interest also continued to grow unabated. The South African *East London* news-paper said that off the field I was 'like any small boy that hangs around a football ground picking up autographs, but when he dons Northern's famous red shirt, the transformation is unbelievable'.

I had already decided that the timing was not right for me to move to one of these professional clubs, but if I continued to make this kind of progress in my career, then the opportunity that suited would eventually arrive. I was not concerned – I knew that I *would* become a professional player. In the meantime, I watched and learned, taking the many opportunities I had to watch professional players at close quarters. In that way, I realised the standards that I needed to reach. I had the opportunity to watch professional players in Pretoria where there was a team called Garrison. It included three players from Airdrie and Sunderland, as well as Dundee's Alfie Boyd. He was a legendary figure on Tayside and was renowned as the captain who won most winners' medals with the Dens Park side. There were other opportunities too. During the Second World War there were many British servicemen stationed in the country and there were a number of professional footballers among them.

The players were not solely restricted to the services. South Africa had also become a popular country for touring sides from Britain after the war and in 1945, Charlton, Huddersfield, Aberdeen, Clyde and Motherwell all visited. The country provided the tourists with a good climate and some competitive football, but these were not the only reasons that British clubs came to South Africa. With all of the home-based footballers strictly amateur, the leagues provided a good breeding ground for players ambitious to turn professional and ply their trade in Britain. Over the years there was a fair number who made the transition successfully into British football. Among them were Herb Currer, Dougie Wallace and Billy Strauss (Aberdeen), Bill Perrie (Blackpool), Sid O'Linn, Stuart Leary, John Hewie and Eddie Firmani (all Charlton), and Alfie Ackerman, Ken Hewkins and Roy Davies, who all played with Clyde. There was also a player called Billy Arnison, who played for a team in Glasgow called 'The Rangers'. The only time I had heard of this team before was from my old coach Alex Prior, who talked of them in glowing terms. However, they had never been one of the touring sides, so I did not think much of it, other than they were obviously a team that had attracted players from South Africa.

With so many British footballers either playing or coaching in South Africa it seemed almost inevitable that I would end up playing football in Britain. However, if I was generally acclaimed, and was confident in my own future, I did not convince everyone. One of the British managers who was particularly keen on the talent available in South Africa was Charlton boss, Jimmy Seed. He was restricted from spending much money by the Charlton board of directors and saw South Africa as a country where he could secure some talent on the cheap. He said that he had turned to South Africa as the war had left Britain short of talented young players, and established British players were expensive to buy. There were no transfer fees to pay to South African clubs as they were not yet fully professional and he said that he could bring them to the UK – 'just for their boat fare'!

Seed was often credited with 'finding' Stanley Matthews, although he did not sign him, but if he was impressed with the great Stoke City and England winger he was less enthused about me. Since I was becoming more prominent in South African football and Seed had taken a few players back to Charlton with him, he was asked by the press why he was not taking John Hubbard. He replied that I was 'too small for British football'. Perhaps he did have a point – in 1949, when I was 18 years of age, I was 5ft 6in and weighed just 8.5st. Ironically, Scottish football was to become famed for a succession of great wingers, all around my size or smaller. However, I was undeterred by Seed's view. He was entitled to his opinion and there were enough who did not share it.

By now, I had switched from Berea Park to Arcadia and then to our local rivals Municipals. I was happy at Berea Park, but the standard of the players at the other clubs was better and I thought that my chances of being picked up would increase if I was in a better team. Although I was still young, I thought I had learned about as much as I could at Berea Park and I needed a new challenge. Arcadia was a fitter, stronger side and had many players I knew from my time at Berea Park including Ken Hewkins, Alf Ackerman and John Hewie. I enjoyed my time there, but I was looking to progress a bit further.

Municipals were highly rated in South African football and had such a good reputation for breeding talented players that they attracted a number of scouts. Indeed, some of their players went on to become good professionals. I felt that they were the ideal side where I could perhaps showcase my talent and that I had to get into that team. However, I could not simply turn up at Municipals and ask to join them. They were the local council's side and the only way I could play would be if I worked for them. I enjoyed working in the sports shop, but I knew that if I was going to play for Municipals, I would have to change jobs. So, with a heavy heart, I went in to the shop to tell them that I was leaving. It was my third job in just over a year and the only one that I enjoyed. I shut the till, put my last box away in the shop, and then prepared myself for the only position available to me with the council – a labourer on Pretoria's roads. As I picked up a shovel then set to work on the city's pavements, I thought, 'What a contrast from the shop!' It may not have been the most glamorous job going, but I saw it as a necessary sacrifice and part and parcel of my apprenticeship towards a future in the game.

With each of these moves there was one role that I maintained – penalty taker. As I moved up every level, the pressures naturally increased with the importance of the competition and the standards, but I did not feel any different as I stood behind the ball. It was always a one-to-one battle of wits between me and the goalkeeper. I had to try to disguise my intentions of where I would place the ball and he had to guess what I would do with it. I was confident every time I took a penalty and with each one I was tasked to take with Berea Park, Arcadia and Municipals, I increased both my confidence and experience. I cannot recall missing any in these early days.

In 1948, as the football season closed and the playing fields at Berea Park and elsewhere were opened up to cricket, my attention switched to the bat once again. I had played cricket for the Pretoria team, before I had turned my complete attention to the Berea Park football team, and I enjoyed playing cricket down at the park in the summer. The games had been typically unorganised, but some of the boys decided we should start our own cricket team – Pretoria Pirates – and I was appointed captain. Considering that our little team was thrown together in a few weeks in the summer, we were very successful, winning our first seven games, during which I scored six centuries. Again, we received considerable coverage in the local press and the comments were resurfacing that, despite my progress in football, I perhaps had a future in cricket.

Although we had formed just a few weeks earlier, we did receive coaching from Reg Perks, who was a first-class cricketer and who had decided to spend the summer in South Africa. He played for Worcestershire and had once been England's opening bowler. He was one of the most revered names in the game at that time and his statistics were impressive with over two thousand wickets to his name. He offered me a contract to play with Worcestershire County Cricket Club, but by then I was also receiving indications of possible offers to play football in Scotland from Aberdeen and Clyde. Nothing concrete was forthcoming from either of these, so I had no decision to make with regard to these two clubs, but I had already decided that I did not want to play full-time cricket. I declined the opportunity to play with Worcester, knowing that someday a suitable offer would come in football. I would not have to wait long before I would have a decision to make – though not from any of the football clubs that had previously shown interest.

I have explained that my ambition was always to play professional football, which might imply that I was interested in the financial rewards of being a player. However, professional football to me was merely a title that indicated the highest standard that I could attain. Money was never important to me, although there were reports suggesting that there were substantial sums moving around the game in the UK. One report at that time featured an interview with Billy Arnison, who was one player with whom I was to eventually have a great affinity. Billy, like many South African players at the time, had moved to Scotland in 1945, just after the war. The newspaper reported that he had joined a team called The Rangers Football Club, or just 'Rangers' as they seemed to be known. He had only remained there for a couple of years before he left to join Luton Town. He came back to South Africa for a short holiday in 1948 and I read an interview that he had given to the local press. He said that many players in Britain were now exchanging hands for £24,000, which, by any standards, was a huge sum of money. That caused quite a stir in South Africa, highlighting that there was obviously a lot more money in the game in the UK. I was not so interested in that, as his experience as a footballer who had obviously done well in the UK. If I was to emulate him and follow him into the professional ranks, it would inevitably mean leaving home.

By 1949, any reservations about being too young to consider a move to a professional club had all but gone. A couple of years earlier I had declined the opportunity to play with Huddersfield and I imagined the offer might still be there if I contacted them. I had also heard that Aberdeen and Clyde were hovering and with the way things were going, there might be others. I knew that the time could soon come when I would be offered terms from a club that I could not turn down. For that to arise, I would have to confront the reality that besides the attraction of playing the game at the highest level, fulfilling my long-held dream, I would need to leave South Africa. Billy Arnison and all the others who had pursued a career in football had to make that decision to emigrate westwards, away from the country of their birth. I would be no different.

While I waited to see what the future held for me, two of my friends received offers from professional clubs and decided to join the exodus to Scotland. Ken Hewkins was a great goalkeeper and he had attracted the attention of Clyde. They offered him acceptable terms and he joined Alf Ackerman who had spent the winter at Shawfield a year earlier. I contemplated the possibility of an offer coming from Aberdeen or the prospect of a chance to join Hewkins and Ackerman at Clyde. As I waited, considering that these two clubs were the most likely to come in for me, another offer came literally out of the blue from my old coach, Alex Prior. I understood that he was representing Rangers, the same team that Arnison had joined. Although I had heard about some of the Scottish teams that had travelled to South Africa, I never really knew much about Rangers, other than what Prior had mentioned and, of course, the Arnison connection. If I knew a little about them, the name Celtic meant nothing to me at that time!

Alex Prior had kept tabs on me and I knew that he rated me as a youngster with potential. I found out that when he coached me at Berea Park, he had written a letter to a Scottish newspaper, *The Sunday Mail*, saying, 'A young outside-left in the team I coach can keep heading the ball 300 times. I have seen him take it round the ground two and a half times. This youngster would hold his place in any first team at home. He has two wonderful feet and has already been tapped by several English clubs. Won't leave the Union for another year though!'

Even when I left Berea Park, Prior had followed my career and, importantly, had the links at high level within Rangers that would open up the chance for me to go to Ibrox. He had watched my development as a player at first hand and he had seen the frequent speculation linking me with a move to other clubs in the United Kingdom. It was only later that I found out that he had recommended me to Willie Allison, who was sports editor of *The Sunday Mail*. Aside from being a journalist,

Allison was also involved with Rangers and was a good friend of the manager, William Struth.

Alex Prior and William Allison effectively acted as agents for Mr Struth at that time and orchestrated the opportunity for me to join the Glasgow side. I still have the letter that Willie Allison sent to Alex Prior on 7 June 1949, confirming Rangers' interest in me. It reads, 'I have been in touch with Bill Struth, and he says he shall be delighted to give Hubbard a chance of playing for Rangers. Keep it under your hat as I want the scoop of it. Rangers will pay his passage here, and in the words of Bill Struth, "The boy will be well looked after while he is with us." If he makes the grade, he will, of course, be well paid by the Rangers, but if he fails to come up to their standard, they will see to it that he has his passage paid back to South Africa.'

It is strange to read of people carving out my future, but what a future and what a club. When Alex Prior first raised the possibility of me going to Scotland a year earlier, I had politely declined the interest. I was simply not ready to move and I believe that the decision was right at that time. At 18, however, with a further year of experience in football and importantly, more personal maturity, I considered that I was ready. Prior explained to me how big a club Rangers was and that the other prospects of Aberdeen and Clyde faded in comparison. The opportunity to go to Glasgow and play at their Ibrox ground was immediately attractive. I was offered £100 signing-on fee and a wage of £12 per week, return flights, and a three-month trial with my digs paid. After the years of contemplating a career as a professional football player, I now had a decision to make – a life-changing decision, but frankly it was easy. It was a good deal and I did not have to think much before accepting, although I still had to speak with my family and get permission from my mom.

When I sat down with mom to explain the offer I had received, she told me that she was pleased and that I should go and show them what I could do. I was excited at the prospect of playing professional football in Britain, but I had a heavy heart. I knew that with my brother and three sisters all married and living away from home, mom would be alone if I left. However, she knew that I was following my dream. She had nurtured and watched me grow up to become mature both as a person and as a sportsman. I was not blind to the realisation that it would be a challenge in many ways, but I was ready for it and she knew that this day would come. She did nothing to try to dissuade me, because she wanted me to live my dream, although there must have been great sadness in her realisation that I would leave. I would face a challenge that would take me into a land that I knew little about – one very far away and 'out of Africa', my homeland.

That evening, I went to bed excited about what lay ahead of me. Mom did not share her feelings as she went to her room that night contemplating my journey to a distant Scotland. I imagine she was probably excited for me and while my aim was to secure a permanent move, we both took comfort in the knowledge that the contract was for a limited term. After all, the terms stated that the trial would last three months and that period would soon go by. We were not blind to the possibility, too, that the deal could be extended. I told her that if they kept me longer, I would send for her.

The offer from Rangers was great news for me and I have no doubt that it also brought some joy for her, but it was tinged with a little sadness. The house in Tulleken Street that was once so lively with seven in the household, each busily getting on with their day, had gradually become quieter. When I left, only she would remain and that must have been very difficult and lonesome. Her children had all flown the nest, but I am sure she would have been comforted in the knowledge that every one of us had settled into quite independent and happy lives. In my case, it was premature to assume that I would succeed in Scotland and the prospect of a return after three months was unwelcome, but nonetheless some consolation as I gathered my clothes. The decision to leave for Scotland had been made and the time was almost upon us.

The news of my offer from Rangers quickly hit the sports pages in South Africa and *The Sunday Times* reported, 'It is the opinion of ex-professionals who have played in Britain that there is nothing to stop Hubbard finding his way quickly into the first team.' The newspaper also wrote, 'He is not unlike Alan Morton… both in physique and the way he goes to meet the ball.'

That one must have made Jimmy Seed take notice. He felt I was too small for football in Britain, but here was I being compared with a man of even smaller stature, who had played on the left wing for Scotland and who earned the nickname of 'The Wee Blue Devil' after torturing the England defence through the 1920s and 30s.

The newspapers also talked of the great players I would line up alongside in the Rangers team including

73

Torrie Gillick, 'George' Thornton and Willie Waddell.
I could not have corrected them by saying 'George' was
'Willie' and Torrie was Torry, because I had not heard of
these players or much about the Rangers for that mind,
but they would become great team-mates. That I did
not even know much about the club just added to the
excitement. The Scots people I knew told me that I was
going to the 'famous Glasgow Rangers' and felt that this
was the best club for me. It was good enough for me – I
could not wait to see them.

My last game in South Africa was, fittingly, for
Municipals against my old side Berea Park. The result
was incidental to the farewell cocktail party that they
held in my honour following the match. The chairmen
of the two clubs each delivered a nice speech with warm
words of gratitude and good luck wishes. I was sorry to
leave both clubs behind as the pair of them had been
important in my development, but I was excited about
the trip to Scotland and what lay ahead.

On the eve of my departure from South Africa, I
went home and organised my case, packing my football
boots along with my clothes, ready for the journey
next day. When I turned in for the evening and went
to bed, I did not realise that it would be the last night I
would spend sleeping in that room and in that bed. To
be honest, I never thought much of it because I still had
it in my mind that I would return three months later.
Leaving Pretoria, South Africa and my mom did not
seem quite so final, but in reality a new chapter in my
life was about to begin – in a new land.

Before I left, I received a telegram from Berea Park
Football Club, saying, 'Happy journey and best of luck in

your new career.' It was a nice gesture from the club that started my career and where I had enjoyed many happy times playing football. However, a day after I left there was to be a second telegram delivered to my home. It came from my father, who I had not seen or heard from in about eight years. It read, 'Cream always rises to the top. Am confident you will succeed in your new sphere. Good luck my boy and best wishes, Dad.'

I was surprised and pleased to receive the telegram, but I would have been more pleased if he had not left us in the first place. I could never bring myself to forgive him for the way he treated us and, in particular, my mother. However, it was a nice thought to send the telegram, even if it did surprise me. Perhaps he was showing some sign of remorse, but as it was winging its way to my home, I had already gone. He was in the past and I was ready to find out what the future would bring.

I was booked on a plane to leave Pretoria's Jan Smutts Airport for London near midnight on 17 July 1949. Even as my suitcase sat in the hallway on the day of my departure with everything apparently cut and dried on my trial at Ibrox, there was another unexpected twist. Clyde's representative, Roy Davies, came in very late and offered me £1,000 signing-on fee, a wage of £20 per week and a two-year contract. It was clearly a much better deal than the terms offered by Rangers, but I had given the club my word and accepted their offer so I could not possibly go back on that. I felt I had a duty to them since they had come along first and, as I said, none of this was really about the money for me. If I had been more money orientated, I would have taken the Clyde offer for sure. But, I was taken by all that I heard about

75

Rangers and excited about the prospect of going there. My instincts were ultimately proven to be correct.

I was accompanied to the airport by mom, my sister Daisy and her husband Charles, who used his car to carry us the 40-minute trip. As expected, the emotions were mixed with some sadness, but I was excited. As I left them and headed to the gate, I turned to wave goodbye. I do not mind admitting that there were a few tears before I marched up the stairway and on to the plane. As I took my seat on the aircraft, my mind had already switched from my life in South Africa to the new adventure. Soon I would be in the air, leaving behind the jacaranda trees for a new climate, a new town and a new life. I was nervously excited, but this was my opportunity and I intended to take it.

5

Arrival At Ibrox – My Blue Heaven

AS the plane took to the skies leaving my family and home behind, my mind was already nervously contemplating this great opportunity. The journey to London took 23 hours so I had plenty of time to think of the future, but my thoughts occasionally drifted back to home and the past. The images of my family, Berea Park, Tulleken Street, and all of my friends flashed through my mind as I gazed out of the cabin window on the night sky. I pondered my memories of the people who were most important to me – a mother who was my best friend and three sisters and a brother who loved their baby John. Then there was Martha, the guardian angel who was my constant companion through my formative years. I also reflected on Berea Park where my true love for sport was nurtured. However, I was conscious that I could not dwell on the past and would now have to look forward to the future and the great opportunity which lay before me.

I contemplated the 6,000 miles ahead to a new continent and a new country and wondered what would await me. I realised that I had been presented with a real chance to make something of a career in football and I resolved to work hard to make sure that I seized the moment. I was not nervous of what lay ahead, but I was curious about what it would be like – the country, the people and above all, the standard of football in Scotland. I knew that the game would be played at a higher level than in South Africa, but I wondered how big a gulf there would be in the quality of the players. Despite the confidence I had in my own ability, I also wondered if I would be up to it and if I was doing the right thing. Those 23 hours were a kaleidoscope of emotions, but dominated by hope and expectation.

When I arrived at London International Airport on Wednesday 18 July, I was met by a representative of Thomas Cook who had been told, presumably by Mr Struth or Willie Allison, that absolutely no one was to see or speak to me until I arrived in Glasgow. There had been speculation in the newspapers before I left that Reg Perks was going to meet me and try to persuade me once again to go to Worcestershire County Cricket Club, at least during the close season. Cook's travel representative stayed with me for three solid hours as we went to the domestic flight terminal, before he saw me off safely on the flight to Glasgow. The weather in London had been very warm without a cloud in the sky and the flight to Scotland had been great with lovely clear skies – until we crossed the border. During the flight, the pilot announced, 'The clouds you see out of your window – well, that's Scotland!'

As we began our descent for the arrival into Glasgow, the butterflies in my tummy also announced their arrival. I'll never forget my first sight of Scotland as the plane banked on our approach to Renfrew Airport. As I looked out of the window, I saw the River Clyde sprawling out across the estuary and the banks flooded with large cranes. From what I could see, Glasgow looked very different and nothing like Pretoria, the city I loved and had left behind. Not good, or bad – just different.

When the flight landed, I quickly disembarked, stepping on to the tarmac and setting foot in Scotland for the first time. I headed towards the terminal building where I had been told that I could expect to meet Mr Struth, the manager of Rangers, at the arrivals gate. I grabbed my bags as they were delivered from the aircraft and headed towards the gate. There, I saw a very smartly-dressed gentleman, who turned out to be Mr Struth, approach a big, athletic-looking American chap in front of me. The young man shook his head and it was apparent that there had been a case of mistaken identity. As he walked away, I reached the smart gent who, by now, I had realised was the famous Rangers manager. I said, 'Mr Struth – I am John Hubbard.' At 5ft 6in and 8.5st, I was obviously smaller than he expected. I thought he was going to have a heart attack with the shock! We exchanged pleasantries and then headed out of the airport, to where Mr Struth's chauffeur – a man named Tom Petrie – awaited. He drove the manager and I to the St Enoch Hotel in Glasgow. On the way, Mr Struth told me that we would have dinner there and then I would spend the evening at the hotel, before being picked up by Mr Petrie in the morning. He said that he would then drop me off at my digs, which they had organised for me near the football ground.

We had a very pleasant evening when Mr Struth told me a bit about Rangers and asked about my time in South Africa. After dinner, Mr Struth said that I was to report for training on Tuesday at 10am prompt. I would use the next day to get settled into my digs, but I asked if I could I go into Ibrox the day afterwards, the Friday, and do some light training, which he thought was a good idea. I had travelled a long way and I was eager to see this stadium I had heard all about. Besides, I had nothing else to do in this strange city. That night, I went to sleep quickly with little time to ponder my introduction to Mr Struth and Glasgow. However, my adventure was about to begin in earnest.

The Scottish press were obviously alerted to my arrival and called Bill Struth to find out about the boy they had heard was 'the best winger in South Africa'. The Rangers boss said, 'As a schoolboy he played inside-forward, but [he would] be content on the wing – it's a lot easier there!' He obviously had some misinformation on my position – I did not play inside-forward, but at least he knew where to play me. Although the club had been looking for a good left-winger for a number of years and had tried the likes of Jimmy Caskie, Jimmy Duncanson and Charlie Johnstone, the feeling was that they had never replaced the great Alan Morton from all those years before. Alan Morton was a small and quiet man, but a huge legend in Rangers folklore. He was Bill Struth's first signing and he went on to play

532 games and score 136 goals for the club over 13 seasons. However, that only tells part of the story of a man they called 'The Wee Blue Devil' after he terrorised the English defence in a match in 1928 – one of a record 11 Home Internationals he played against them. He had also won nine championships and three Scottish Cups and had become a director at Rangers.

Morton set a tough benchmark, but I was just a youngster and I knew I would have a long way to go before I would have the chance to even play, let alone try to emulate this great man. I first had to impress to win a contract, but the shadow of the likes of Alan Morton loomed large.

Although Morton was a director and was at Ibrox throughout my career, one of the disappointments of my time at Rangers was that I rarely spoke with him. I had always felt that since he had played in the same position as me, he could have given me the benefit of his huge experience.

Perhaps it was simply down to the fact that he was a quiet man, but I always tried to make new arrivals welcome at Ibrox in later years. It was what I had experienced from the majority of people I had come into contact with at the club and, even today, I like to have a chat with the new players when they come to Rangers. I think it is good to be able to pass on a little advice based on experience, whether it is taken or not.

On the Friday, I went to Ibrox as arranged and when I first saw the ground with its huge red brick façade, I thought it was just out of this world. I could not believe that this was the ground where I would now play my football. How different it was from Berea Park, back home in Pretoria. I was mesmerised with the whole situation. I could not believe how quickly things had happened and the magnificence of this arena that stood before me. I had come 6,000 miles to play for Rangers – a club I had barely heard of and now, here I was at their stadium. As I walked up to the impressive front door, I saw the mosaic at the entrance with the club's crest in red, white and blue. As I stepped on to it, I was met by the imposing Rangers trainer Jimmy Smith, who stood 6ft 3in and weighed 17st. I peered up at him, not realising that Smith was once a Rangers legend himself – a man who had also played centre-forward for Scotland. After his playing days had ended he had been offered the opportunity to join the ground staff by Mr Struth and was obviously one of his trusted lieutenants. He showed me to the dressing room, which was off the main hallway, along a corridor. When I entered the dressing room, I was immediately impressed. It was wood-panelled and much bigger than I had been used to. It has not changed to this day and I can still remember when I first walked into it.

Mr Smith handed me a neatly folded grey shirt, black shorts and a pair of brown football boots then said, 'Get stripped and go and enjoy yourself with that ball.' As I changed, I laid my clothes on the bench and put on the shorts. I noticed that they were much longer than I had been used to, reaching halfway down my legs to below my knees and towards my ankles. I thought that either they did not have players as small as me or perhaps all the players at Rangers were giants. Certainly if they were anything like Jimmy Smith, I would be in a very small minority!

When I was ready, I picked up the ball and walked out of the dressing room, then ran across the underground track beneath the stand, down through the tunnel and on to the pitch. Before, and laid out in front of me, was this wonderful stadium. Wow! I looked around at the vast terracing sweeping up from the pitch. Behind and above me was the huge grandstand with row upon row of seats. I was taken by the enormity of it all. I didn't know at that time that the stadium had once held 118,000 people for a match against Old Firm rivals Celtic, but it would not have surprised me. Little did I know that I would eventually score a New Year's Day hat-trick against them inside this ground, when it would be filled almost to its capacity, but more of that later.

Although the players never generally trained on a Friday, there were some around the stadium that day who had come in to receive treatment for injuries or were trying to get back to full fitness. The first player I met on the field was Ian McColl, a real gentleman who was to eventually become a team-mate and a good friend. He was just a few years older than me and had joined the club from Queen's Park four years earlier. He had already established himself in the team, but he had sustained a leg injury and had come in to Ibrox for some treatment. After exchanging pleasantries in our introduction, off I went, with the ball at my feet. Glasgow was alien to me, but I was very comfortable on a football field and I was always at home running around the grass with a ball. I ran and ran, all over the pitch, just occasionally stopping to keep the ball up with my feet and head. Then I would stride down the wing and cross the ball to an imaginary centre-forward. I took lots of corner kicks with my left foot and my right, and of course, had to run to get the ball each time. I even took penalty kicks – scoring, then running behind the goal to collect the ball. It was merely a rehearsal for a routine that I would follow many times more in the future, only then the goalkeeper would collect the ball from the back of his net. I was bursting with enthusiasm inside this great stadium and immediately felt at home, although I was many miles away from Pretoria.

After an hour on the pitch, I went for a bath and then Jimmy Smith came in to tell me that 'the Boss' wanted to see me in his office upstairs. I changed and, for the first time, climbed the imposing Marble Staircase which dominated the hallway and ended at the manager's office. The first thing that caught my eye as I climbed the stairs was a large portrait on the wall of a fine-looking footballer. I learned later that it depicted Alan Morton – the man who once played in the position I coveted. I thought of how great a club this was that celebrated its best players in such a way. It was future player-manager Graeme Souness who once said that Rangers was a proper football club and his comments mirrored my own perspective as I walked up the stairway.

At the top, I walked across the corridor to the manager's office and knocked on the door. I heard Mr Struth call 'come in' and when I walked into the room, he was seated imposingly behind a big desk. He asked me to take a seat and then he said, 'I was in the directors' box watching you and you will do me just fine. I'm signing you on for the rest of the season.' He gave me a £300 signing-on fee, which was treble the amount initially promised and told me that my trial period would take me through the full season, rather than the three months originally offered.

I was excited to sign the contract that he had put in front of me and I was delighted that he had arranged a photographer to be there to capture the moment. I was now officially a Rangers player and I could not wait to get the chance to play. With the formalities concluded, Tom Petrie whisked me off in the club car to my new digs with a Mr and Mrs Kelly, who lived near Ibrox. The couple had looked after many players when they first arrived at the club and I learned that both fellow South African Billy Arnison and Willie Thornton had also lived there.

It had been a whirlwind 24 hours when my feet hardly touched the ground. I had left South Africa just a day earlier with dreams of a professional career in football, but still conscious that I may return home before the winter had set in. Perhaps my mom expected me back at the end of my three-month trial but I had impressed Mr Struth enough to guarantee my stay for at least a full season.

Signing that extended contract was a huge boost to my confidence and any doubts that I had about succeeding at Rangers were well and truly dispelled. I reasoned that if Mr Struth had seen enough in me in that short time on the field to consider that I had a chance to break through, then he was probably a better judge than me. He knew the standards that players had to reach to become Rangers players and by extending that contract, he confirmed to me that I had at least a decent chance. I already had confidence that I would make it, but when I saw Ibrox I was even more enthused to make this place my home. I had such a great feeling about this club, with its stadium, Mr Struth and the whole atmosphere of Ibrox that I knew that I wanted to remain there. Above all, I wanted to become a star player at Rangers and to wear the club's royal blue jersey.

I had been fortunate enough to have been spotted by Alex Prior, who lined up this golden opportunity for me to make the grade with a top club and I intended to take it. It was without question that I was hugely impressed with everything I saw at Ibrox. But, if I was impressed by Rangers, then I seemed to have impressed them too. Jimmy Smith told the press, 'I've been a long time in the football game. I've seen promising youngsters in my day. But, if this youngster doesn't make a hit with Rangers fans, I'm willing to eat the boots he is wearing.' South Africa seemed a long way from Scotland but I was completely taken by the club. More importantly, I already felt settled and comfortable there, so much so that I wanted it to be my new home.

I was comfortable with my digs at the Kellys', which was a good base for getting both to Ibrox and the city and I quickly settled in to life in this new world. The first few days with Rangers and in Glasgow were something of a culture shock, but as I got to know the people around Ibrox, it seemed that everyone I met at the ground was very friendly. One of those I got to know very well was Willie Dinnie, who worked on the ground staff. Rangers Football Club has always had people who have committed their lives to working at the club and Willie was one of these stalwarts who worked quietly in the background.

He invited me to his home for tea and when I got back to the Kellys' after training, I got changed and headed out towards the Dinnies' home. As I headed down Shieldhall Road, wearing my white shorts and a light coloured t-shirt, I became conscious that a number of people were staring at me. I must have been a comical stand-out to them, because although I dressed as I normally would back home in Pretoria – this was not South Africa. Then I noticed that everyone was either carrying a raincoat or wearing one…but it was a summer's day. I was to find that this was quite typical of Glasgow – a grey city where the people seemed to accept that if it was not raining, it might rain eventually. Later a rain shower duly arrived and I realised that this climate was not perhaps what I was used to. I knew then that I would have to dress like the Glaswegians, which would mean a complete overhaul of my wardrobe.

I had a lovely evening in the Dinnie household – the first Scottish family I had met. We chatted about South Africa and they filled me in with more background on Rangers and the other players. Over the next few weeks I built up a good relationship with the Dinnies' oldest son Bill, who worked part-time at Ibrox along with his father. Bill and I were to become lifelong friends.

The next day I continued my adventures in this strange new place, by taking my first tramcar into the town. Although we had trams in Pretoria, I had never seen so many in a city. It seemed that if you missed one, another would be along in a minute, sometimes with two and three in succession. It was just part of the different culture I would experience in these early days. Glasgow also had a bit of a reputation for being a tough town back then but I never sensed any fear or had any concern as I made my way around. My impression of the city was that it was big and very old, with many open spaces where buildings once stood. I had assumed that these had been the result of bombing which had pounded parts of the city during the Second World War which had ended just four years earlier. However, Glasgow was also in the midst of slum clearance with new buildings emerging, amid the older Victorian properties and shops. These older buildings cut quite a contrast with my native Pretoria, where the properties were generally newer. After all, Pretoria was no more than 100 years old at that time, but Glasgow had been established centuries before. If it was a dark industrial city, it was also vibrant and I found the people to be very friendly. Although I felt that the city had lots of people, it was actually quiet when I arrived. I had heard that almost 250,000 had left at the weekend on what I was to learn was the start of Glasgow Fair fortnight. It would get busier, of course and soon I would see Glasgow as it would normally be after the Fair, with the streets of the centre thronged with people.

Although it was the close season, the team still trained and I had joined them on the Tuesday for my first official training session as a Rangers player. There I met up with many players who were already household names in football throughout the country. They included George Young, Willie Thornton, Willie Waddell, Jock 'Tiger' Shaw, Bob McPhail and Jerry Dawson. At that time, the names did not mean anything to me, but I quickly learned that the whole team had already attained great fame in footballing circles. They had won many trophies for Rangers over the years and when I joined the club, they were still wallowing in a unique success – the first domestic treble of the league championship,

Scottish Cup and League Cup. They could easily have been aloof and detached from me, but they were all very welcoming to this young lad from another continent. I had changed in the dressing room just a few days earlier, but with the room full with the entire squad, they took the opportunity to show me around once again, highlighting the great sunken bath and the showers. I had met Ian McColl on my first visit to Ibrox, but over the next few weeks, I would get to know all of the players; especially the reserves such as Duncan Stanners and Minty Miller, with whom much of my early time at Ibrox would be spent.

I could see that all of the players had taken their traditional places in parts of the dressing room. I looked for an available space and placed my things on the bench. High above me on the wall were odd-looking pegs which I struggled to reach. I learned that these pegs were quite famous for their curious shape, extending out from the wall and designed to hold a bowler hat. The players in the early years used to wear bowlers, which set them apart from those who played with many other teams. I was also to learn that Rangers players had to be smartly dressed at all times in what was something of a tradition perpetuated by Mr Struth.

We were expected to maintain such high standards in everything we did and good dress sense and smartness were important to the man they called 'the boss'. I did not wear a bowler, but I still had to reach the peg to hang up my jacket and shirt. The only way I could reach it was to stand up on the bench and, as if to emphasise my lack of height, when I looked around the dressing room, I noticed that no one else had to. Over my time at Ibrox,

I was one of the few who had to stand on the bench to reach the peg.

In these early days training was always at Ibrox, although later in my career it switched to the Albion training ground, opposite the stadium. As I was getting ready, I was conscious that the other players must have been wondering if I would be any good.

Training was a routine to them, but this day was huge to me. It was hardly make or break, but I was aware that first impressions are important and I wanted to ensure that I made my mark. I was very focused as I ran out on to the Ibrox pitch to begin that first session. I always trained hard throughout my career, because I was a 'wee man'. With the words 'a good big 'un is always better than a good little 'un' resonating in my ears, I was always keen to show that my small stature would not limit my capabilities. I had that determination to show that I was at least the equal of a bigger man and it had always been a factor in my game, which extended to training too. In this, my first training session with the club, I was particularly focused to show that I could be an equal to all these great Rangers players.

While many decades have elapsed since that first training session, I have no trouble in remembering what we did on the day, for one good reason – it never changed in all my time at Ibrox. Training was always held on Tuesdays and Thursdays and we were required to get to the ground and be ready in time for a 10am start. Then, we would all go out on to the field together, where our two trainers, Jimmy Smith and Joe Craven, would take control. If they were not on the field with us, they would sit in the dug-out and watch, firing out instructions as we came past. They were accompanied by two capable assistants – Jimmy Smith's dogs, Sandy and Mac! The routine began with circuits around the pitch – walk a lap, then run a lap, walk the bends, then run the sides, do 20 sprints, then finish with a seven-a-side game behind the goals.

We rarely saw Mr Struth on the field at training, although he would occasionally peer out from the directors' box, just as he had done when he saw me on that first Friday. I understand that in the early years, he used to join the players on the field for a walkabout, but age had caught up with him and he seemed to prefer catching a glimpse from the stand. The running track had been his domain, as he had once been a reputable athlete, but as an old man in his 70s, he was by then more comfortable in the stand or in his office.

As I went through the routines, I was conscious that all of the eyes were on me in that first session and in the seven-a-side game which we played behind the goals. I was unaffected and got on with things, playing as well as I could and working hard as I always did. Training always finished before 12 noon, when we would head back to the dressing room to get bathed and changed, then head home. By the end, I had some satisfaction in the belief that I had done well and the reaction, although hard to judge, seemed pretty positive. It was to be the first of many happy days I enjoyed in training at Ibrox, and the routine never changed in all the time I was at Rangers. I always enjoyed training, but I would say it was not as rigorous as the work we put in back in South Africa. In fact, I felt I was fitter with the training I received at Berea Park than I was at Rangers.

What immediately struck me about Rangers was that it seemed to be a club with strong traditions which appeared to be ingrained within its fabric. Although the tradition of bowler hats for the players had been dispensed with long before, we always had to be smartly dressed with a collar and tie on matchdays. Indeed, as I mentioned, whenever we represented the club, or turned up for training, we were required to be well-dressed. These were the standards Mr Struth expected of every Rangers player and there was no compromise. He established standards that he expected the players to adhere to and part of the adjustment in these early days was understanding what was expected of me. I learned very quickly that we also had to follow strict codes of behaviour.

We were not allowed to swear or drink while on Rangers duty, and he hated smoking. That did not curtail me, however, as I used to have a cigarette before every match – in the toilet cubicle. That was to be a routine for other Rangers players in the future, including Willie Johnston and Paul Gascoigne who would use the same cubicle! In fact, I used to smoke 30 to 40 a day, but if Mr Struth knew I was smoking, he never mentioned it. It was probably a case of, 'Do it if you want, but don't let me see you doing it!'

Things at Ibrox are rather different nowadays and players have the freedom to walk around all areas without restriction. However, in my day, there were areas within the Main Stand that were out of bounds for us. We were mainly confined to the ground floor, which is where the gym, the dressing room and boot room were, but we were not permitted to go up the marble staircase to the upper level dominated by Mr Struth's office, the boardroom and, of course, the Blue Room. An exception was when we were summoned to the manager's office, or when we were given some latitude to go up to play snooker. The snooker table has now gone, but it was once the centrepiece of the room we now know as the Trophy Room. I always find it quite ironic that for all the trophies Mr Struth won, he never saw the Trophy Room as it is now. The change in its use took place three years after he died.

While Mr Struth is often credited with introducing these strict standards of dress and behaviour, I understand that they probably originated with the first manager of the club, William Wilton. However, Mr Struth was dedicated to maintaining the standards of the club as he had quite high ideals for what he expected of a Rangers player. He always wanted the best for us and we knew that we had to abide by the high standards he set for us to be good enough to be Rangers players.

I settled in to these traditions quite easily and there is little doubt that we did feel quite special being Rangers players at the time. My career was in its infancy, but I was always conscious of Mr Struth's guiding hand as I was nurtured in the early stages. When my signing was first announced to the press, Mr Struth told them that he would allow me 'to acclimatise and then to graduate from the reserves into the first team'. It was clear that he had some expectation that I would make the grade – but not immediately. For all that it was encouraging that he seemed to have some expectations that I would succeed, I realised that I would have to go through an apprenticeship as a player.

I had been aware of my football apprenticeship as I worked my way through the system from Berea Park to Municipals and now, at this higher level, I realised that I would have to continue that progress. I had no difficulty in accepting this, as my more immediate concern was to settle down to this new life at Rangers. With my first training sessions out of the way, I was confident that I had done enough to show the rest of the players what I could do, but I wanted to show everyone else that I could play. I was excited by this new environment and I looked forward to the time when I would get the chance to represent the club in a competitive match in front of a decent crowd inside this great stadium. I found that I would not have long to wait for my chance.

6

The New Ranger

I MUST have impressed in my training sessions, because on 6 August 1949, just three weeks after arriving in Scotland, I got the chance to pull on the Rangers jersey for the first time. The Ibrox Sports, as it was known, was a top-class athletic meeting held every year generally on the first Saturday in August. Bill Struth had been hugely influential in the success of the Sports, travelling far and wide to court the best athletes and persuade them to come to Ibrox. Olympic and world champions would regularly appear and even Olympian Eric Liddell, celebrated in the movie *Chariots of Fire*, had at one time been a member of the club and ran at Ibrox. The sports meeting traditionally attracted huge crowds who were not, however, simply there for their interest in athletics. A five-a-side football knockout tournament, which generally featured the best sides in the country, ran in tandem with the athletics card. For most of the fans though, it was a chance to see their team in the summer and get a glimpse of the new players who would feature in the coming season.

The tournament was played on the full pitch and Rangers invited seven teams to join them – Celtic, Clyde, Hearts, Hibernian, Partick Thistle, Third Lanark, and Queen's Park. The matches were played on a knockout basis. It would be my first opportunity to wear the royal blue jersey and when the moment arrived, I felt good when I pulled it over my head. As I looked out on the stadium, I was amazed at the big crowd – 60,000 of them – and their passion! My first reaction was, 'What a lot of people have come for the athletics!' They had not come solely for the athletics, of course – they eagerly anticipated and supported the new players and I was one of them.

As our first game kicked off, I quickly learned that five-a-side on a full pitch was very different from the full 11-a-side game. With fewer players on the vast playing surface of Ibrox, there was much more space, but also much more running to be done. I had never played 'fives' before and I very soon realised just how big the pitch was. Determined to do well, I was all over the place and did not pace myself. Looking back, I was probably over-eager to impress, so at the end of the first match I was shattered, although we had won. I had run myself into the ground in the first few minutes before I realised that you should only use your legs when your brain told you to – not your heart. However, I am a quick learner and I settled down in the next game with most of the big crowd urging us on.

We fought our way through to the final where we would face a good Hibernian side and I think I had played quite well in helping us to get there. I was not selected for the final, with the five players that were chosen coming straight out of the team that had won the treble, but it was great to be involved. Mr Struth was clearly keen to ensure that another prize was added to the three trophies that already sat on the boardroom table. The Rangers side included Jock Shaw, Ian McColl, Willie Findlay, Willie Thornton and Willie Waddell – all household names. The Hibernian line-up had Jimmy Cairns, Willie Finnigan, Jock Paterson (whose son Craig once played for Rangers), Bobby Johnstone and Willie Ormond. Rangers won 1-0 and, as part of the winning team, I received a set of cutlery as a prize, which I sent back home to mom shortly afterwards. Even though the event at The Ibrox Sports was just a five-a-side competition, I felt that it had provided me with a great introduction to competitive football at Rangers and that I had come through it well.

Having played in front of a decent crowd and represented the club in this short game, I now looked forward to playing in a full match. That opportunity was to come just a couple of days later with what they called the 'trial night'. This was a regular fixture which featured a game between the first team (Blues) and the reserves (Stripes). It was held on the Monday after the Sports and in the week leading up to the first game of the season. It was a regular feature in the Rangers calendar until the 1960s, and I think it is something that the club should look at introducing again. It gave the fans a chance to see the new prospects coming through and also provided the players with an opportunity to show what they could do. I was not the only new player in the trial match. Willie

McCulloch, who had just signed from Strathclyde, was another player who was making his debut. Willie went on to play a good few games through the 50s and became a good team-mate.

As one of the new players, I was selected for the reserve team, in my favoured outside-left position in direct opposition to big George Young, or 'Corky' as we called him. Young was a colossus of a man who was also something of a legend with Rangers and Scotland, who he captained. Although he was a good bit bigger than me, I was unconcerned with his height or his reputation and I looked forward to the match in front of the 12,000 crowd that had turned up at Ibrox. After just five minutes I got the chance to get into the game when I took a pass and then began to advance up the wing. As I approached Corky, he moved towards me, then stood, legs astride, to block my progress. Because of his size, his legs were so wide apart I could almost have crawled through them. However, I slipped the ball between them, then ran around him on his right side. Nothing was said! I think he was a little startled and a few minutes later, I got the ball again, advanced toward him and did the very same thing – again running around on his right. As I passed this time, he said, 'Is that the only trick you know?' It was partly in jest, but he obviously wanted to test me out. I said to him, 'I'll let you know in the second half!'

In the second half I gathered the ball again and he approached me in the same formidable way. This time, I slipped it through his legs and then ran around his left side. As I went past and he floundered, I said, 'Is that better?' He mumbled something under his breath, something unrepeatable, but it was all good banter. We exchanged a few words when the ball was away and I told him that I knew a few more tricks, but I would save them for the opposition. These kinds of exchanges are fairly typical of what you get in a football match and you have to be able to deal with them. Most of the players had a good sense of humour and this was fairly typical of the banter on the pitch every time we played.

The exchanges with Corky were fun, but the game had provided me with an opportunity to show what I could do against a great player who was a hero for both Rangers and Scotland. In my mind, if I could show that I could play well against the great George Young, then hopefully it would demonstrate that I could perform against anyone. Certainly, I felt I had played well and after the game, Willie Waddell told the press, 'After he gets used to our short passing game, he will be a master.' That was important to me and gave me a boost, because Waddell was a winger himself, with both Rangers and Scotland, and he knew the position. Trainer Jimmy Smith also had some kind words to impart to the press and said, 'Hubbard would be one of the outstanding personalities in Scottish football this winter. His ball control verges on the fantastic.' It seemed that I had made my mark, even to the extent of drawing comment from the press. The *Glasgow Herald*, under a banner headline of 'Ibrox Recruits Promise', reported my 'commendable display', praising my 'clever, intricate footwork'.

The Stripes lost the game 2-0, but we put up a decent performance against the more experienced Blues team and should have probably drawn that match. The first goal was down to a defensive lapse from Duncan Stanners, who scored an own goal when trying a backpass. Ironically, our team also lost the opportunity to level things when Jack Lindsay missed a penalty, which Bobby Brown saved easily. There would come a time when I would be trusted with the Rangers penalties, but there would be many more missed by others before the ball would end up at my feet.

The victory was sealed for the Blues when Willie Findlay got the second. There were some decent players in the Stripes team including George Niven, Johnny Little, Willie Rae, Willie McCulloch, Torry Gillick (as a late substitute) and Billy Williamson. The Blues side was familiar to those who knew the great Rangers team of the 1940s. It included Bobby Brown, George Young, Jock Shaw, Ian McColl, Willie Woodburn, Sammy Cox, Willie Waddell, Willie Findlay, Willie Thornton, Jimmy Duncanson and Eddie Rutherford. The core of Rangers' great team remained and, although I expected that I had shown enough in the trial match, I knew that I would have to content myself with a place in the reserves at the start of the season. Our opening match of the season would be against our great rivals, Celtic, so there was no prospect of me playing in that game. Eddie Rutherford would play on the left wing for the 1949/50 season and I would have to learn to 'acclimatise' in the second string until Rangers – or more particularly, Mr Struth – considered that I was ready.

I got the opportunity to play in another fives competition just a few days later when the Scottish Amateur Athletics Association games were held at Ibrox, also culminating in a football tournament. This time I played all the way to the final, although we were shaded out by Partick Thistle. Playing in the reserves in these early days gave me the opportunity to settle into life at Rangers and also to play with some great players, learning from their skills at close quarters. One of the players who was hugely influential to me in these early years was Torry Gillick, whom I played alongside in my first four reserve games. He had joined Rangers in 1933, playing his first game when I was just two years old. He was at Ibrox for just two years, before being transferred to Everton, but he returned to Rangers as a guest during the war years before completing his transfer back to the club. He had been a favourite of Mr Struth and featured in some of the great matches through the thirties and forties, winning cup and championship medals. Torry was a great player who was very comfortable on the ball and could see the pass. We formed a great partnership together, with Torry at inside-left and me on the wing – a wing partnership that brought me seven goals. However, it was not all good. On one occasion – my second reserve match – both Torry and I had a game that both of us would want to forget.

We faced Queen of the South at Palmerston Park and we were losing 1-0 with just ten minutes to go, when the ball went out for a throw-in. I ran to collect it near the barrier, when an old fan of the Dumfries side said to me, 'Away back to South Africa ya black b*****d!' Getting barracked by the crowd was something every player has to contend with, but I was riled in that instance. I picked up the ball and gestured to throw it at him, but didn't. The referee saw it and promptly sent me off. I felt really aggrieved because it was me who had taken the abuse and I had not thrown the ball at the fan, although he certainly deserved it.

Torry said to me, 'Don't go off,' and I said, 'But I have to – the referee has sent me off.' He repeated, 'Don't you go off!' but I realised I had no option, even though it was a ridiculous decision. I trudged off the park, down the tunnel and into the dressing room. Disgusted, I took my gear off and then went into the bath to soak. Five minutes later, the door of the dressing room opened and Torry appeared. Probably still aggrieved at my dismissal and unhappy with the referee, he had got involved in an incident with the Queen of the South right-back and both were sent packing.

Even the press were bemused by the incident and one pundit commented that it was hardly serious, assuming that there were also words exchanged, but there weren't. Regardless, the SFA did not see it that way and I received a two-week suspension for 'striking a spectator with a ball', which I didn't.

Mr Struth sent a letter to the SFA disapproving of the referee's handling of the game. It was fairly typical of him – always looking to protect his players, particularly when there was a sense of injustice. He was never slow to take things up with the football authorities if he felt that we, or Rangers, were being unfairly treated.

Just five weeks after arriving in Scotland, I had my first experience of an Old Firm match – on this occasion from the Main Stand, as a spectator and not a player. I had learned from everyone around Ibrox all about the intense competition that existed between Rangers and Celtic, but I had never experienced the intensity of the fixture first-hand. It seemed that for weeks in advance, everyone was speaking of the game – a League Cup tie – and the players looked forward to it. From the build-up and the tension in the week going into the game, I could see that this was a special fixture.

When the matchday arrived, the setting was ideal with the weather glorious and very hot – much more like I had been used to in South Africa. There were 95,000 inside the ground just before the match kicked off – the biggest crowd I had ever seen assembled anywhere. As I sat in the stand and looked around at the magnificence of Ibrox with its packed terraces, I was completely enthralled. This was what football was all about and the atmosphere was electric with the incessant noise resounding throughout the ground. The stage was set and the game was to prove to be a good one for Rangers, although very eventful.

It was extremely competitive and in the early exchanges, Celtic were on top and continued to dominate for much of the first half, playing towards their own fans on the western terracing. Rangers' Sammy Cox, an uncompromising defender, played at right-half that day. Celtic's inside-forward Charlie Tully was a tricky player who was popular among the away support and he liked to be on the ball. After about 30 minutes, Sammy put in a tackle on Tully in front of the away support. The referee waved play on, while all of the Celtic fans believed that it should have been a foul and some action taken against Sammy. The place erupted with all hell breaking out among the Celtic supporters. There was an avalanche of bottles hurled from their fans into the Main Stand, where the Rangers supporters were seated. The Light Blues fans were trying to protect themselves from the hail of glass, then out came the mounted police. Three mounted police took their horses up into the terracing to the area where the bottles were being thrown from and order and arrests soon followed. As the match neared half-time and with most eyes on the terracing, watching the melee unfold, Willie Findlay scored to put Rangers 1-0 ahead. That simply added fuel to the situation.

Ten minutes after the restart, with tempers frayed and emotions high, Rangers were awarded a penalty when Willie Waddell was cut down in the box. That caused further disturbance in the Celtic end as all eyes again switched from the field to the terracing. George Young stepped up, but rattled the ball off the bar and it was cleared. I wanted to be down on that field and taking the responsibility at the penalty, but I knew my time would come. By now, the Rangers team was in control of the game as the pace slowed due to the searing heat. The events on the terracing also seemed to have had an effect on the match as the challenges became less intense.

With less than ten minutes to go, Willie Waddell scored the second for Rangers and the victory was effectively sealed. Waddell had switched to centre-forward in place of the injured Willie Thornton, who had retired with a broken bone in his foot. That just about finished the game and when the final whistle went, we had won 2-0, but WOW! What a baptism into the world of the Old Firm. It was certainly nothing like I had seen before, but an exciting game – both on and off the field.

Rangers ended up winning easily, playing with a free-flowing attacking style. The team's defenders were attackers long before the term 'wing-back' was to be used in coaching manuals and we had some great players who could get forward from deep positions. It was the passion of the game that amazed me, however. I laugh as I write this thinking that Graeme Souness was once quoted as saying that an Old Firm victory in the league is just worth three points. I am sure it was just tongue in cheek, because these games are much more important than simply the points. In the aftermath, one newspaper suggested that if the disorder was going to continue at these games, then the teams should wear different colours. They suggested that Rangers might wear red and Celtic black and white! Thankfully, sanity prevailed on that one – Rangers will always be blue and Celtic green, but the tension never left Old Firm matches and I loved them.

Celtic were upset with the refereeing that day and requested an SFA enquiry, which ultimately led to both Sammy and Tully being censured. The referee also received a warning, though his problems were more down to his inexperience of the fixture.

The Rangers team that day included Bobby Brown; George Young, Jock Shaw; Sammy Cox, Willie Woodburn, Willie Rae; Willie Waddell, Willie Findlay, Willie Thornton, Jimmy Duncanson and Eddie Rutherford. Each of these players was a star in his own right and most were Scottish internationals. They had also carved their own piece of history in winning that first treble. I realised that they would all be hard to displace, but I knew that I would get a chance and I was excited with the prospect that I would join these great players in the same team. I longed for the day that I would play regularly with them, especially against Celtic.

Many of the players were at their peak when I arrived and Eddie Rutherford, who held the outside-left position, was just 28. There seemed no prospect of him retiring in the next few years, so to get a place in the side I realised that I would have to earn it, by showing I was better. Although I was enjoying playing in the reserves with the likes of Torry Gillick, I was ambitious and very keen to get my chance. That opportunity to wear the royal blue jersey in a proper first team match would surely come, but when, I wondered?

7

A New Adventure
In An Old City

HAVING played a few reserve games and represented the club in the fives in front of a big crowd, I was desperate to play in the first team. I made no secret of my feelings at training and both Jimmy Smith and Joe Craven were aware that I was itching to get a chance. I imagine that they had a few words with Mr Struth because he summoned me to his office one day after training. As I sat in the room, he looked up from his desk and told me that he was aware of my enthusiasm to play with the top team, but it would depend on who my direct opponent would be. He explained that he wanted to play me, but only when he thought that I would get a clean game from the opposition. He was obviously concerned that, with my slight build, I might be roughed up by some of the more physical players in the league. Although he offered me no timescale on when I would get an opportunity to play with the first team or even commitment that it would actually happen, I felt that my big day was not so far away. Looking back, I realise that I was impatient and that he would have been quite entitled to send me packing. After all, I was just a youngster and had barely arrived at the club.

A short time later, Mr Struth called me up to his office once again and said that he had decided that he would put me in the side to face Partick Thistle at Ibrox on the coming Saturday, 10 September 1949. He reckoned that I would be in direct opposition against the Jags full-back Jimmy McGowan, who he believed would give me a fair, clean game. McGowan had been with Thistle for eight years and had been capped for Scotland so he was a decent player and a fair one by repute. Setting aside my excitement, I knew that it would be a difficult contest for me, even if the Boss thought it would be a clean contest. I reflected that it had only been seven weeks since I had arrived from Pretoria and here I was about to make my full debut. Eddie Rutherford stepped down to make way for me on the left wing and, with Willie Thornton ruled out with a broken foot, Billy Williamson came into the side to take his place. I had played alongside all of the players at training, of course, but I was thrilled as I took my place in the dressing room, ready to play alongside these Rangers greats. The team announced that day of my first team debut was: Bobby Brown; George Young and Jock Shaw; Ian McColl, Willie Woodburn, Sammy Cox; Willie Waddell, Willie Findlay, Billy Williamson, Jimmy Duncanson…and me.

All of the players in the dressing room were aware that it was a big day for me and came up individually to wish me well before the match. One of them, Sammy Cox, who played at left-half and would be behind me on the left wing, offered me some great advice. He said, 'I'll look after you. Just do the easy thing – pass!' Sammy's advice was both good and sensible. I was ready! I was full of pride as I ran across the indoor track, down the tunnel and then on to the pitch. You have no idea what a wonderful feeling it was for an 18-year-old from South Africa to run out in front of over 70,000 roaring fans.

As I lined up, Jimmy McGowan, who as expected was in direct opposition to me on the wing, came over and shook my hand, saying, 'Just go out and enjoy the game.' It was a great gesture from a true gentleman. From the kick-off, the game became something of a blur and seemed to fly past. It was a good all-round performance and we won 2-0, with two first-half goals from Waddell and Findlay. Mr Struth had been correct in his assessment of McGowan. He did play the game fairly and I enjoyed my match against him. I felt I had played well and I was eager to read the press reports the next day – they made very pleasant reading. The first I read was in the *Sunday Mail* and written by journalist Willie Allison who had been so influential in my move to Scotland.

In his coverage of the game, he wrote, 'If South African Johnny Hubbard can find plenty of grub in the cupboard and add a stone or two to his well-knit eight and half stone frame, there is no reason why he shouldn't become the football equivalent of golf's Bobby Locke, but he is awfully wee. He bounced off Jimmy McGowan in the physical contact and Jimmy was scrupulously clean like a pea blown against a rubber bag. Yet he [Hubbard] is good and loaded with intelligence. No doubt about that. Particularly with his slide rule passes and accuracy in the cross. It wasn't so much what he did himself as what he made others do that caught my fancy. Rarely attempting to beat his man in the dribble, he'd short pass the ball to Duncanson or back to Cox, run and wait for the return. True, he needs experience but [it] will come if he can provide the rest. It is too early to pass final judgement but I think he's got what it takes.'

On the Monday, Alan Breck of the *Evening Times* said, 'Without a doubt Ibrox had taken little Hubbard to its heart. His slips to Duncanson after holding the ball and making sure of the position of his partner were most refreshing. I wondered if the South African would be the last contributor to the return of intelligent forward play in Scottish football.'

These were encouraging words and although I did not score on the day, I had a hand in both goals. The press noted I had played a 'team game', passing the ball around rather than taking men on. I had followed the good advice that Sammy Cox had given me and it worked well. Although I felt that I had fitted into the side well, I was under no illusion that my appearances would be limited at this stage. Just three days after the Thistle game, Rangers were scheduled to play Celtic in a Glasgow Cup semi-final tie and I knew that I would not figure in that game. As expected, Eddie Rutherford came back into the side and I was reconciled to the likelihood that I would have to wait some time for another chance to play in the first team.

As it turned out, I did not have to wait too long for another chance to pull on that royal blue jersey. Just three weeks after making my debut against Thistle I was selected to play for the first team once again, in an away league fixture against Falkirk. Willie Waddell was left out of the side and Eddie Rutherford switched to the right wing, from the left, to fill the gap. I came in to take up the available berth on the left wing, where I faced a full-back called Jock Whyte, who was something of a journeyman pro. I played well enough and we won the match 2-0, but it would be six months before I would get another opportunity to play in the first team. Perhaps they felt I was still too light, or otherwise not ready for a run in the side. I realised that there were lots of well-established players at the peak of their careers ahead of me, so I had resigned myself to the fact that I would have to be content with reserve team football for the foreseeable future. At least I had got my Ibrox career off the ground, but I knew that I had to continue my apprenticeship. I did continue to press for a place in the team with some good performances in the reserves where I played 17 games and scored 11 goals. I knew that I would get another chance, but now was the time to build my experience.

My first few months at Rangers had been a bit of a whirlwind. I had settled in at Ibrox and with a couple of first team games under my belt, I had every reason to be happy with how my career was progressing. However, by October, I became homesick. I had built up some good friends, but life as a professional footballer left a lot of free time and probably too much time for me to think. It is a common problem for many footballers, especially those who are unmarried. With training ending at around noon each day, it leaves a lot of spare time. But for me and the players around Ibrox in those days it was worse, because we did not train every day. In my spare time, when I got back to my digs, my mind would wander back to life back home in South Africa. It seemed like homesickness, but on reflection now, I do not think that it was. Rather, I feel I was probably just bored.

With training restricted to two mornings a week, I found that the Tuesday and Thursday afternoons were empty and on Mondays, Wednesday and Fridays, when there was no training, I was completely at a loose end. Some players, like Ian McColl, were in part-time employment, so boredom was never an issue for the likes of him. However, most of the others had to learn how to contend with the empty days, and they would look around for ways of filling in the time. Many could be found on the golf course, but the game was weather dependent and, in any case, I found the idea of playing at a course three times a week tedious in itself. I did not feel that I was particularly good at golf, even though my handicap was 12, but I suppose this was fine for a left-hander playing with right-handed clubs!

Like some of the others, I played a lot of snooker and we all managed to reach a good level. I became quite proficient at the game, playing in the billiard room at Ibrox after training or in a snooker hall in West Nile Street. I think the building is still there, but it is now used as a nightclub. If there were none of my friends around I would still go down to the hall to practise. One day I was practising on my own, when the door suddenly blew open, like a scene from a Western film. Through the glare of the light I could see the silhouette of someone standing there – a wee man, indeed, smaller than me. I asked him if he wanted to play and he responded, mimicking my accent, suggesting that I could have three blacks of a start. I told him that he could forget about that as we racked up the balls ready to start. He continued to mimic me as I suggested that the loser should pay for the table. He accepted, still mimicking my accent, and broke the balls, sending them all around the table. I set about potting and built up a lead, before giving him a good hiding.

Through the match we chatted and I quickly learned that his name was Joe McGill and that he was just 17 days younger than me. He worked in a nearby timber shop and, if we were not matched at snooker that day, or indeed any other time, we became, and remain, great pals. He could not come to games on a Saturday because of his work, but I invited him along to some midweek matches at Ibrox and even after I left Rangers, Joe followed my career and came to some matches.

There were some players who were not so interested in either snooker or golf and the most notable of these was Torry Gillick. He was one of life's characters and his interests lay in the mysterious world of the greyhounds. If you could not find Torry, he would invariably be at the greyhound track. Torry loved his dogs and would always amuse us with some great stories about his experiences as he travelled around the tracks of Lanarkshire.

Whatever the players' preferences were in the way of recreation on their days off, the majority also had family that they could go home to each day. This was one of the things I struggled with early on in my time with Rangers. I was largely alone, except for the people I had met around Rangers or a few friends from South Africa, who, like me, had joined Scottish clubs. Make no mistake though – I do not mean that I stayed at home every night! If we filled in our time during the week playing football, snooker and golf, we had other pursuits in the evenings – girls!

When I lived in South Africa, I had a girlfriend, but it was not a serious relationship and we did not keep in touch after I left. In Scotland, I was young, free and single and quickly learned of the best places where I could meet young ladies with similar interests – dancing! I loved dancing and there was no shortage of good dance halls in Glasgow. I usually went along with the likes of Ken Hewkins and Roy Davies, who were friends with that common bond of being professional footballers from South Africa – and all looking for a girlfriend. We all knew each other from our days back home and would meet up on a Thursday night at the Locarno Ballroom, in Sauchiehall Street, which was one of the most popular places in the city. The format at the Locarno was always the same – the girls would stand at the back of the ballroom and the boys would assemble at the front. As the music played we would walk to the back and ask a girl to join us on the floor.

One Thursday evening, on 13 October actually, things began to look up when I met a very pretty girl named Ella Black. I picked her up for a dance and then another and another. We both got on well that evening and as I said goodbye and left for the evening, I was already looking forward to meeting her again on the following Thursday. We met up at the Locarno once again, as arranged and we eventually began courting. Footballers can often attract girls through their celebrity status, but even though I was a Rangers player, it had nothing to do with Ella's interest in me. She knew nothing about football so she was probably quite unimpressed when I told her I played for the club. However, Rangers has an irresistible lure and eventually, she would really get hooked on football, to such an extent that she would never miss a Rangers game home or away. Even today, she often joins me at matches at Ibrox.

Meeting Ella was to become so important to my wellbeing and comfort in Scotland. We dated as often as we could, although we lived at opposite ends of Glasgow. I lived in Drumoyne Drive in Govan, in the west of the city, and getting to Ella's home in Sword Street, Dennistoun, was a bit of a trek. I had to get the subway from Govan underground and then jump on a tram to reach Ella's home. As our relationship began to build I decided to get a flat, at 521 Duke Street in Dennistoun, to be closer to Ella. While it cut down my travelling to see her it left me a long awkward journey to get to Ibrox for training. I came up with the idea of getting a bicycle, so I went into Glasgow on the Monday and bought a lovely bike. The next day, I proudly took to the streets and cycled into Ibrox. When I arrived at the ground, Jimmy Smith took one look at the bike with horror and said that the Boss would frown upon it. He advised that I should get rid of it before Mr Struth saw it as he did not believe that cycling built up the right muscles for football. So, the next day, with my tail between my legs, I sold it. Today I find it funny thinking of the bike I bought on the Monday, rode on the Tuesday and then sold on the Wednesday!

Ella filled a big void in my life, but she was not *always* there and I was still keen to fill in the remaining time on my days away from Ibrox. I realised that I could not rely on golf, snooker or Ella to fill every day, so I decided to try to get a part-time job. Considering my experience in Pretoria, I thought that my best chance of work would be if I could get into a sports shop. I had enjoyed working in the sports retailer back home and it was certainly more interesting than working on the pavements or in the railway office. I looked around and saw one shop in Argyle Street, under the railway bridge – the Heilanman's Umbrella as they called it in Glasgow. It had been the traditional meeting place for people from the Highlands in Scotland who had settled in the city, so it was perhaps ironic that, as an immigrant, I should seek work there. I went along one day, popped in and approached the owner, whose name was Russell Moreland. I learned that he had been a football player himself, before becoming a manager of and then a director of Third Lanark Football Club. The conversation went something like this:

'I am a South African looking for a part-time job over the Christmas period.'

'That's a long way to come for a part-time job,' he replied.

'I have another job but it leaves me with too much time on my hands.'

'What's your other job?' he asked.

'I play for Rangers!'

He told me that he had already decided to give me the position even before I had mentioned my other job, but that this had been the clincher. I enjoyed working in Mr Moreland's shop, and although it was not the kind of place that attracted fellow football professionals, we did occasionally get other sports celebrities. One such visitor was boxer Vic Herman with whom I was photographed in the shop, in advance of one of his fights at Hampden Park. He obviously got the right gloves from us because he took his opponent out in the first round after that picture was taken. Herman, who was born in Manchester but brought up in the Gorbals, was considered by many to be the best flyweight to come out of Scotland and not win a world title. They called him the Jewish Bagpiping Flyweight because he would pipe himself into the ring and made bagpipes as a profession. He was an interesting character.

The homesickness I had for a short time had gone and I began to feel that life was beginning to fall into place for me. I had a great new girlfriend, my own flat and a career that was developing very well in the sport that I adored. I loved being at Rangers and working for Mr Struth, who was a kind of father figure to the players. He had built the standing of Rangers and he was fiercely protective of the club and his 'boys'. He ensured that only the best would be good enough for us and there was always a feeling that he watched over us. Perhaps he was conscious of the free time we had, but he would often take us away from the city in between games, staying at a nice hotel and enjoying some relaxation with our team-mates. These trips helped to build morale within the player pool and demonstrated the status of the club.

Just after I started working at Moreland's sports shop, I heard the other players talking of one of these upcoming trips, which I learned was planned for the Turnberry golf course and hotel. I gathered that Rangers went there quite often and it seemed to be quite a place, from what they were saying. I was looking forward to seeing it and to playing on a course that had already established itself as one of the best, even though it had not hosted an Open Championship at that time. Although I wanted to play the course, I only had an old set of clubs. I imagined that the other players would be well kitted out so I did not want to get embarrassed. I felt that I should probably get a new set before I went down to Turnberry. Moreland's shop did not stock any golf clubs, so I went down to another sports outfitters that specialised in golf equipment – Lumleys in Sauchiehall Street. They had a good selection and I got a lovely brand new set of clubs with a bag.

When the day of our trip arrived, we travelled by train from Central Station down to Turnberry. It was my first trip to this famous resort hotel and it was all that I had expected. We were to make many more trips to the hotel in my career with Rangers, when the itinerary would almost always be the same. We generally travelled down after our match on a Saturday and, following our check-in at the hotel, we would usually all sit down to dinner. Next morning we would head the short distance down to the course for the first of two rounds of golf on the Sunday. These were followed up with another two rounds on the Monday, one round on Tuesday, then after lunch, we would return to Glasgow.

After a pleasant night in the hotel on that first evening, we wandered down to the first tee on the Sunday morning. Jimmy Smith was organising the groups and announced the players in teams of four, until there were only three players left – Jock Shaw, Torry Gillick and me. Gillick and Shaw were yet to appear from the clubhouse, but we were to be the last group, so there was no rush.

As I stood there with my new bag and clubs, watching successive four-balls leave the first tea, I waited patiently for my playing partners. Eventually they appeared and Jock Shaw came out of the clubhouse first. Over his shoulder, he was carrying an old ladies' golf bag which was full of holes and inside the bag, there were about four or five clubs – all different. Behind him was Torry, with no bag and carrying just one iron over his shoulder. My first reaction when I looked at him was that he must be some player if he can go around Turnberry with one club! We had been grouped in the one and only three-ball and what a unique one it would be.

With all of the other players gone, we teed off. Having seen the previous groups tee off at the first hole with mixed fortunes, I had a little more confidence that I would not embarrass myself on the course. I could see that for all that my team-mates were great footballers, they were not exactly great golfers. Through our game, Torry hit every shot with an iron, from tee shots, bunker shots, to pitches out of the rough and even putting.

It was a long round and we arrived back at the clubhouse just as the first of the afternoon four-balls was about to tee off for their second round. When we finished, I totalled my scorecard and had an 89. Jock had actually played reasonably well and he worked out that he had a 98. Then Torry announced that he had scored his card at 137. I said to him that I did not think that his arithmetic was right, to which he announced that it was his first-nine score! However, there was more to our game than could be assumed from the simple scorecard. I had lost eight balls, Torry had lost five, and, although Jock had lost just two balls, he also lost a club at the first par three! This was no ordinary game of golf. One memory of Torry's performance that day was when he played one shot from the side of a bunker. As he swung at the ball, he lost his balance, fell and rolled down the hill. After we had lunch in the clubhouse, there was no time for another full round so we played pitch and putt in front of the hotel instead. At least there was less chance of Jock losing any more clubs or Torry rolling down any more hills!

If the golf was fun, it was not the reason I had come to Scotland. I was at Rangers to play football and was eager for another taste of first team action. In May, seven months after I had last appeared in the team, I was recalled to play in the Charity Cup semi-final against Partick Thistle at Ibrox. We won the match quite easily, 4-0, with Jimmy Duncanson scoring the first goal, before Willie Thornton went on to score a hat-trick. I had a good game, this time against Peter Collins, not Jimmy McGowan, and Mr Struth decided that I had earned my place in the team for the final at Hampden, three days later. That final would be against Celtic. It would be the last match of the domestic season and my first match against the Parkhead side. I was desperate for any first team action, but to get a game against the club's biggest rivals was beyond my dreams. The Charity Cup was not the greatest prize in Scottish football, but any Old Firm game inspires fierce rivalry and competition. A crowd of 82,000 gathered inside the national stadium to watch this clash of the giants – and one little winger.

I had watched from the Main Stand when the teams had clashed back in August and I recalled that the atmosphere was electric. Then, the stadium was like a cauldron of noise and I was excited with the prospect of going out into that kind of atmosphere.

Despite the importance of the fixture, I had no real nerves, just excitement as I waited inside the dressing room until it was time to take to the field. When we were given the nod, I proudly ran on to the field. The wall of noise hit me – what an incredible atmosphere! I was so excited and who could not be, running out on to the pitch at the national stadium in front of such a crowd? The match was completely unlike anything else I had experienced as a player. I sensed the hostility within the ground immediately and when I went near to the Celtic support, I could hear them booing. It did not trouble me at all and, if anything, their catcalls probably inspired me more. I reasoned that it probably highlighted that I was playing well. I would have been worried if they were not giving me a roasting, which might have suggested that I was not doing my job. If that had happened, I would have been as well walking off the park, but it didn't.

As it turned out, the game was not to be memorable from a Rangers viewpoint, but it did have a touch of Hollywood glamour. Film star Danny Kaye was introduced to the crowd and to each of the teams before the match. He was also supposed to kick off, which on these occasions was an honour often accorded to celebrities. In the warm-up he was up to all sorts of antics – playing with a piper's busby, then doing his own little Highland fling in the middle of the park. We stood by watching this circus, while trying to concentrate on the game ahead. He then knocked the ball out of the referee's hands, and kicked it ahead of him, before dribbling all the way towards our goal. Our goalkeeper Bobby Brown stood aside to allow him the luxury of scoring into the empty net. Instead, he blasted the ball past the post and to this day I am not sure if he just miscued, or if he deliberately missed through fear of causing a diplomatic incident.

If Danny Kaye didn't score into our net, Celtic did manage to get the ball past Brown quite quickly. Unfortunately, Willie Woodburn and Sammy Cox succeeded where Kaye failed – in putting the ball past our own keeper. In fact, these two own goals helped Celtic race to a 3-0 lead before we pegged the score back to 3-2, but we just could not get an equaliser despite pressing incessantly at the end.

Despite the defeat, I earned some plaudits at the end with one correspondent saying, 'Rangers for once had an outside-left who looked the part. Hubbard is small and light, but knows his limitations, crosses well with either foot and with a Cairns or McPhail at his elbow, might solve an Ibrox problem of long standing.' It was my Old Firm debut, but if I lost that one, I would win many more in the future and gain my revenge on Celtic. I was disappointed to be on the losing side that day, but it was an important game for me. I showed that I could play in the tension of an Old Firm tie and, if the result did not turn out quite right, there would be many opportunities to redress the balance in the future.

The teams who faced each other on that first Old Firm tie for me were: Rangers – Brown, Lindsay, Shaw, Little, Woodburn, Cox, Gillick, Paton, Thornton, Duncanson, Hubbard; Celtic – Bonner, Haughney, Milne, Evans, McGrory, Baillie, Collins, Fernie, McPhail, Peacock, Tully.

Although I had not figured much through the season, it was a great feeling when the club retained the Scottish league championship. It was a tight race right up until the finish when a draw against Third Lanark at Cathkin Park earned the single point that was enough to give the club the title once again. Hibernian, who were our closest rivals in that period, finished just a point behind. In contrast, Celtic had a relatively poor season and finished 15 points behind Rangers, despite edging us out in the Glasgow Charity Cup. The League Cup was also lost when East Fife defeated us narrowly in the semi-final, but later that season we gained some revenge by winning the Scottish Cup with a 3-0 victory over the Methil side. It was a great league and cup double and it gave me a chance to watch at close quarters as the club continued its dominance in Scottish football. It also highlighted the standards that the club was maintaining and the levels of expectation that Mr Struth had established.

On reflection, my first season at Ibrox was all about learning. I was still young and had entered a new country, joining one of the biggest clubs in football. Importantly, I had joined a club with a man of huge influence and control at the helm – Mr Struth. I had a burning ambition to succeed, but I also knew that he would guide my career, just as he had done with all the great players around me. I was impatient, but I also understood that I would need this apprenticeship. I had also learned that this club was an institution and that there were standards to be reached in every sense. I had no doubts that Rangers was absolutely the right club for me. I reflected on the possibility that I could have ended up at Pittodrie or Shawfield. If I had decided to go to Clyde, for example,

I am sure that it would have been a short stay. I would probably have gone into their first team sooner than I did with Rangers, but I was not really ready for the game at that level. If I had been introduced as a youngster and failed to impress through poor performances or over-confidence, my career may have been curtailed. I could easily have found myself on the way back to South Africa. More importantly, my chance to play with a club like Rangers may have gone if I had taken the Clyde offer, or gone to Aberdeen, as seemed likely at one stage. Young, talented, but in a new world, I would have probably gone astray. It is something I have often reflected upon. At Ibrox, it seemed that my whole career was carefully planned out under the watchful eye of a man who was a true Rangers legend.

As I look back on that first season, therefore, I regarded the year as one in which I served part of my proper apprenticeship in the professional game in Scotland. I certainly could not have had better guiding hands than those provided by Mr Struth and his backroom team. I had played for three years in South Africa and had progressed to the highest levels that football in the Transvaal could offer. However, the game was not at the same standard as I had experienced in Scottish football and I knew that I still had a bit to go. Mr Struth was right to nurse me into the game and if I had not received that kind of preparation and care, I might not have turned out to be the same player.

After the season was over, we prepared for an overseas trip to Scandinavia, where we would play three games against select sides including the best they could offer. We left Scotland on the Monday after the Charity

Cup Final, but without Mr Struth who was not in the best of health. It would be a hectic tour as we switched around two countries, but it was an opportunity for the players to unwind after a competitive season. When the flight reached Copenhagen, we then had a six-hour boat trip to Malmo, where we played our first match of the tour against the home side, who were Swedish champions. We won 1-0, although I was not in the side.

Directly after the game was over, we went to a reception that the Swedes had arranged for the Rangers party. This was to be my first real experience of drinking with the other players. When we arrived at the banqueting suite, everybody was given a large glass of the local drink – snaps – not to be confused with the German 'schnapps'. All of the players put a shilling on the table and bet me that I could not drink the whole glass at once. I should have realised that there was more to this game than I imagined! When I drank the contents of the glass, the rest of the players bet that I could not do it a second time, which I duly did. It was only a small glass, so what was the problem, after all?

Gradually, the drink began to take effect. My head started spinning and I could not walk straight on our return to the hotel. On the way we passed through gardens with rose beds on either side of the path. I tried my hardest to keep to the path and away from the rose bushes, but without much success. When I reached the hotel, my trousers were torn and my legs were scratched and bleeding. While I would have preferred to go straight to bed, we were scheduled to head back to Copenhagen, where we would play another two games. We picked up our bags and then headed off to the airport for the

30-minute flight back to the Danish capital. I was totally incapacitated and Jimmy Smith and Joe Craven walked me arm-in-arm to the plane. I did not even know that I was on a plane or remember that I was very sick through the whole journey. I am a quick learner and it was the first and last time I was sick through drink! I suspect that if Mr Struth had been with us, none of this would have happened, but it was good education in any case.

Any chance I had of playing in the next game, two days later, was well and truly gone as I struggled to recover after my introduction to 'snaps'. Our opponents in the first of the double-header in Denmark were Staevnet – a Danish Football Association select side. We recorded another win, this time 2-0. Within a short time I was back to normal and I finally got a chance to appear in a game on the tour when we played Akademisk Boldklub (AB) six days later. AB were the Danish champions and it was the hardest match of the tour, particularly since they had been strengthened with two international players. This time, we lost 2-1, but despite losing, it was good for me to be involved and again I thought I had a decent game. AB were two ahead within five minutes of the interval, but we managed to pull one goal back, and were very unlucky not to get a second. The crossbar thwarted us a number of times and we could not get the equaliser. It was the team's first defeat by a foreign side since the Second World War, but we were not disgraced. We returned home, having seen out a good season for Rangers.

The season also marked the end of my trial period and, while I was a little uncertain if I would be retained, I considered that the club would not have taken me on tour if they intended to terminate my contract. As it turned out, I was offered terms by Mr Struth who confirmed that my trial period had been successful. I realised that I would not be returning to South Africa any time soon and that my future lay in Scotland. Besides, I was very settled with Ella and I had no interest in going back to Pretoria. Glasgow was now my home and I was proud to be a Rangers player.

With the close season came the time to switch off from football and enjoy other recreations. Even though I had come to Scotland to play the game I loved, I did not lose my affection for cricket or my desire to play the game. Earlier in the season, West of Scotland Cricket Club had offered me an honorary playing membership which I had accepted. I could not play while we were in the throes of the football season, but when it was over and we had returned from Denmark, I played for seven weeks before pre-season training commenced. I went straight into their first team and managed to get a few runs for them, so it was a nice opportunity to play competitively in another of the sports I loved. The summer is very short, however, and soon it would all begin again at Ibrox as I moved into my second season.

8

Settled At Ibrox And With A New Wife

WITH that first season under my belt, the three-month contract that become a season contract was extended even further with new terms. I looked forward to the new season at Ibrox with some anticipation, but my optimism and excitement on the future was tempered somewhat by concerns surrounding the health of Mr Struth. The Rangers Sports were scheduled to take place on 29 July 1950, but a week before then, the manager was admitted to the Victoria Infirmary with a serious illness. We knew that he had problems with his leg, but we were surprised when he was admitted to hospital. He was discharged, but re-admitted again in August and at that time, they decided that he would have to undergo an amputation of his leg below his knee. It as a serious and debilitating operation for a man who had been among the fittest, running at tracks up and down the country as a professional athlete. He was now an elderly gentleman, but we realised that the loss of his leg would mean that he would be severely restricted in his work, especially with his office being upstairs inside Ibrox. As a consequence, he became increasingly more reliant on Jimmy Smith and Joe Craven, who would carry him up and down the Marble Staircase. They also took more control of the team affairs and, while most of our time was spent with them anyway, we saw less and less of the manager.

The 1949/50 season provided a league and cup double and had been a great one for Rangers, but the illness to Mr Struth seemed to be reflected in a string of poorer results in 1950/51. The club was very much in a phase of transition at that time, with new players arriving, and my opportunities to play in the first team were becoming more frequent, though not at the start. I still found it hard to break through as they persisted with Eddie Rutherford on the left wing in the early part of the season. While there were some new faces, the season also saw the departure of some players who had been great servants for Rangers. Among those who were to leave that season were Jimmy Duncanson, who went to St Mirren in November 1950 and Billy Williamson, who also went down to Love Street in February 1951.

One of the fresh faces to arrive that season was centre-forward Billy Simpson, who had signed from Northern Irish side Linfield for £11,500 in October 1950. Just after he joined, he got the chance to wear the blue jersey of Rangers for the first time in a reserve match against Queen's Park Strollers at Ibrox. He scored and I managed to get a hat-trick so it was a nice way for us to start off together as team-mates. The good relationship we enjoyed that day on the field continued off the field and eventually on it. One of the reasons that we got on so well was that we always considered ourselves to be the two foreigners in the team – me from South Africa and Billy from Northern Ireland! Billy and I were to become great friends, playing lots of golf, and we remain so today, although age is now taking its toll on him.

Rangers stuttered in the early part of the campaign, while I continued to play with the reserves. At the beginning of December, a defeat from Clyde was the sixth suffered by the team in just 21 games as they slid to mid-table. Rutherford sustained an injury and I was drafted in to the team to play against Morton a week later for my first game of the season. We won the match and I played quite well, but a cold snap of weather with snow and frost prevented any football for a further two weeks. It ruined any chance I had of getting a decent run and that was compounded by a disciplinary suspension I received from the SFA for an accumulation of bookings when playing for the reserves. That ruled me out of three games over the two weeks of the busy festive period, during which time I missed an Old Firm match, which we won. Although I came back into the side when my suspension was over, I was soon relegated back to the reserves when Rutherford was restored to the left wing.

Despite missing some games through the weather and then my suspension, this enforced break from football was actually welcome in one respect. It coincided with a period when my mom visited from

South Africa. Since I was now well settled in Scotland with no prospect of returning to South Africa in the near future, I brought her over for a holiday. We stayed in a lovely flat at 28 West End Park Street, in the West End, near the university which was ideal and gave her plenty space of her own. She stayed with me for six months through Christmas and New Year, right up to the spring and we had a wonderful time. The weather may have disrupted the football card, but it gave her the chance to throw snowballs for the first time in 40 years!

Before my suspension kicked in, I was selected for the first team again for a match against East Fife, just two days before Christmas. It was quite special because I scored my first goal for Rangers – and not from the penalty spot. The goal was not spectacular, but it was still a goal and if it was a personal triumph for me, it was particularly memorable for Billy Simpson. Although he had played twice before for the first team, he had not managed to get on the scoresheet and had been kept out of the side by Billy Williamson. He seized his chance this time, however, and scored a hat-trick.

After my suspension was over, football was again disrupted by the weather with the card wiped out for two weeks. When we resumed at the end of January, I played once again in a 2-1 victory over Hearts. I had a reasonable game and it seemed that, if I was not first choice, then the manager was comfortable enough to put me into the side as back-up. The following week, Rutherford was restored to the side and I reverted back to the reserves.

Through the rest of the season, Mr Struth brought in a few younger players. Even though he was beginning to age himself and was ailing with ill health, he knew that the team had to evolve. The club was also linked with a young Ian McMillan, who was making a name for himself at Airdrie, but it was to be another eight years before he would come to Ibrox. If McMillan was an opportunity lost at that time, there were some young players who were introduced, but did not make any impact. Young Rex Dunlop was tried as an inside-forward to Willie Waddell, but he never really made the breakthrough. Another youngster who came into the team was Willie Beckett from Renfrew Juniors, but he never managed to establish himself in the first team either. Willie was tried at the outside-left position, in competition with me and Rutherford, but it did not work out for him. I had not harnessed a regular place in the first 11 myself, but I was really beginning to feel part of the team.

By the end of February, we were adrift in the league and had been knocked out of both the Scottish Cup and League Cup. I found my appearances becoming more frequent as Mr Struth looked to change things around. Then, in March, he signed John Prentice from Hearts as he continued to try to get the balance right. Prentice was a good player who made his debut as my inside-forward later that month, but he did not manage to play many games through the remainder or indeed in the following season. However, he went on to become an important player with the team afterwards and he was a good lad. The changing personnel was symptomatic of the situation at Rangers at the time. The great treble-winning side of 1949, when I arrived at the club, was disintegrating and Mr Struth was trying to rebuild a team that could emulate them.

From the end of March onwards I got a run in the side, but not displacing Eddie Rutherford who moved to inside-forward to accommodate me. Towards the end of the season I played in a 5-1 win over Third Lanark, when Billy scored four of the goals. I did not keep my place in the game against Hibs the following week (when we lost 4-1) or in the Celtic game (which we won) that followed. It seemed that I was being selected for some games, but not the bigger ones. Clearly I still had a bit of work to do to convince Rangers and Mr Struth that the outside-left position should be mine.

The season petered out and Hibernian took the league championship a comfortable ten points ahead of Rangers, who finished runners-up. Having surrendered the Scottish Cup and failed to progress beyond the sectional stage of the League Cup, the only chance of silverware that season was the Glasgow Charity Cup. It was not the most glamorous tournament in the calendar but it was an opportunity to finish the season on something of a high. I played in the semi-final against Third Lanark, which we won on the toss of a coin after the game ended level at 1-1. I did not have my best game and lost my place to Willie Beckett in the final against Partick Thistle, managed by former Ranger Davie Meiklejohn. The team did not play so well, but won 2-0 to at least salvage something from the season.

As the season ended, my mother headed home to South Africa, having had a chance to see me settled in to my new environment. She enjoyed her time in Glasgow and she met many of my friends including the Dinnie family, who had been so kind to me on my arrival in Scotland. Indeed, she had become close friends with

Mrs Dinnie and they had gone out together every week. They both enjoyed their trips to the Empress Theatre in Glasgow where they saw all the top acts that visited Scotland at the time, including a great Scottish comedian, Johnny Victory. Mom had a wonderful holiday and it was good to have her with me in my new home in Glasgow. I would have loved for her to remain but the cold weather was hard for her to tolerate and even though the spring brought some warm air, she was looking forward to returning home to the sunshine of South Africa, her bowls and her garden back home in Pretoria.

Although it had not been a great season for the club, I was feeling much more settled into life in Glasgow and I knew that Ella was the girl that I wanted to share it with. We were seeing each other at every opportunity and we were both very happy. I eventually plucked up some courage and popped the question. To my delight, she said 'yes' and we married at the registry office in the Burgh Chambers in Glasgow on 26 June 1951. Willie Dinnie, who had become the first friend I made when I arrived in Scotland, was my best man. We had our reception in a restaurant in Duke Street in Dennistoun, then enjoyed our first night as a married couple in a hotel at the top of Buchanan Street.

The next day we headed by train to Aberdeen, where we stayed near the Majestic Theatre. It was my first visit to the Granite City although there would be many more in the future and, in particular, to Pittodrie Stadium. We could only stay for a short time as training for the new season started a few days later. Soon afterwards, I got some welcome headlines in South Africa – 'Hubbard Marries a Black – Ella Black'. The following October the first of our three children arrived, a girl called Linda, the loveliest girl you have ever seen. With the arrival of our daughter Linda, I realised that there was little chance that I would ever return to South Africa to live. By now, though, I had already decided that my life would be in my new homeland of Scotland.

Everything seemed to be going my way off the field, although, in football, I was still struggling to make the outside-left position my own. The press talked of the difficulties that Rangers had in finding the right man for the outside-left position but I knew that I could be the answer to the problem if they gave me a sustained run in the side. The close season of 1951 was very short and it would open with a game against Aberdeen in a newly constituted tournament called the St Mungo Cup. The match was to be played at Pittodrie on 14 July 1951, just over a week after I had returned from my honeymoon there. I was listed in the Rangers travelling squad of 14 players, but the press speculation on who would play at outside-left continued. It seemed a straight choice between Eddie Rutherford, John Prentice or me. Disappointingly, Prentice was selected as I had to sit on the sidelines and watch us lose this first round match by two goals to one. I had certainly enjoyed my trip to Aberdeen a week earlier much more.

I had become resigned to the probability that I was not going to go into the 1951/52 season as first choice for the outside-left position. Sure enough, in the early part of the campaign, Eddie Rutherford and John Prentice contested the role as I sat on the fringes. Rutherford played in the majority of the games in the early part of the season, but he suffered an injury in mid-September.

By then, even John Prentice had drifted out of the scene along with Billy Simpson, who lost his place to young Willie Gardiner. The youngster made his debut in the game when Rutherford was injured and retained his place for the next match. I expected to be given the nod in Eddie's absence, but Willie Paton was thrown the jersey.

I was incredibly disappointed and with a league match against Celtic looming, I did not expect that I would be selected for that either. Paton had not played well when he came into the side on the wing, but it seemed that there was a reluctance to play me, especially in the bigger games. At least, by now, I was always in the pool and as I turned up at the ground for the Old Firm match, I was very pleasantly surprised to see my name listed in the team.

It was incredible that the first match that I would play that season would not come around until late September – and it would be against Celtic! I had already played in that atmosphere of course, but not at Ibrox. Prior to the match, both clubs and the authorities had appealed for good behaviour and a ban was put in place to prevent banners and flags. It did not prevent one Union Flag from being unfurled in among the Rangers fans, as the Celtic crowd waved their scarves. I was desperately keen to play well and as the match progressed I felt good. I was up against Sean Fallon and I felt that I had the beating of him.

We went in at the interval a goal down when Bobby Collins scored midway through the first half, but these matches were always open and we were sure that we could get back into the match. In the second half I almost scored when the ball rattled off the crossbar, but a goal from Willie Findlay was enough to give us a 1-1 draw in front of the 85,000 fans. The game was generally considered to be one of the best Old Firm matches and was relatively trouble-free.

Despite my performance, the game never signalled a run in the side for me as Rutherford returned when he regained fitness. At least I knew that they did not see me as a risk in the big games. I realised that there was little I could do other than to continue to work hard at training and perform well with the reserves. Eddie Rutherford had a lot of experience and it seemed that while he was at the club, my opportunities to play in the first team would be limited. However, just a few weeks later, there was a shock in store for me – and Rutherford.

The newspapers announced that he was going to be transferred to Hearts, apparently leaving the way clear for me to get a regular place in the side. However, the deal would involve Colin Liddell making the move west from Tynecastle. Liddell was another outside-left and any hope that I had of moving directly into the side seemed to be dashed by another obstacle. I was a little surprised by the move since Liddell had struggled to maintain a place in the Hearts side and he came in on a straight swap for a player who, despite being inconsistent, was popular at Rangers. It was certainly a further disappointment for me, as the newspapers had already speculated that I might at last get the jersey that I coveted. In fact, it seemed that the door to a regular place in the first team had closed as soon as it had opened.

Liddell went straight into the team and played on the wing for most of the remaining games that season. It would have been a blow to me had it not been for the fact that I faced an even bigger threat to my position at Ibrox.

That threat came in the form of a letter delivered through the post. As a British subject (through the Commonwealth) and being resident in the UK, I was called up for National Service. I had to report to Padgate in Lancashire for two years where I would serve with the Royal Air Force. It was a necessary duty, but it seemed that it would interfere with my career, just as I was trying to make my mark at Rangers. I would not appear in the first team again until May, when I featured in Charity Cup ties at the end of the season. I had come to Scotland to play football and now I was about to find myself in a uniform.

9

Out Of A Jersey And Into A Uniform

CONSCRIPTION to the forces was an obligation that every young male between the ages of 17 and 21 faced in the United Kingdom when I arrived in the country. They were expected to serve in the armed forces for two years, and remain on the reserve list for four years, when they could be recalled for short terms thereafter. Although some men were exempt of National Service, such as those working on what were called 'essential services', including coal mining, farming and the merchant navy, everyone else had to fulfil their obligations. It was not simply a case of enlistment and serving time at a barracks – we could be drafted to anywhere that the army was active. At that time, there were operations to quell disturbances in Malaya, Cyprus and Kenya, so all of these tours were possible. Although I was South African and playing for the best team in the country, I was a British subject and not exempted. To be honest, I did not really expect to be called up, but when the call came to serve in the Royal Air Force in 1951, I was very happy to do so out of a sense of duty and for my adopted country.

From the moment the letter arrived everything seemed to happen very quickly. After Ella got over the shock of my impending departure, I told Mr Struth. The club realised that this was something I had to do, but I got the impression from the Boss that he was pleased. He was a strong supporter of the armed services and I suspect that he felt that a spell in uniform would be good for me. And so it was to be.

I later learned that Jimmy Seed, the Charlton manager who made frequent raids of South African talent, used to send his players home every two years to keep them out of the services. Apparently this was a way around the system for people from the Commonwealth, but if Mr Struth knew how to work the system, he never adopted it. I suspect that he was more interested in his boys doing their duty and I was happy to do so too, no matter the inconvenience.

When the time arrived to leave, I said my goodbyes to Ella and my team-mates before turning up at Central Station and boarding the train heading south to RAF camp at Padgate, near Warrington. It was here that my fellow conscripts and I would be prepared for our spell in the services and where a bit of military discipline would be introduced for those that needed it. There were 30 Scots and me on the train and when we arrived at the camp we were given short haircuts and kitted out in our uniforms.

Padgate was deep in the heart of the Lancashire countryside, but it was a pretty uninteresting place at the time. It was intended to be no more than a transit camp for us and then we were scheduled to head off to another station to do our square bashing for eight weeks. However, when the officer in command at the base discovered that he had a footballer in the group, the plans changed and we were all kept at Padgate. The rest of the boys were not happy with this change in plans, because they imagined more pleasant surroundings or at least a more exciting setting. I am still unsure why he kept us all at the camp – maybe he wanted me to play in the camp team, but the rest of the boys soon got over the shock and forgave me, even though we were billeted in a cold hut.

That winter was particularly cold and after completing exercises and drills, we would spend the evenings all huddled together around a single coal fire, desperate for some heat. This was the routine, although one evening I got a little too close to the fire. I found myself getting very hot and then I discovered that I had burnt a hole in my trousers! Next morning, I was put on a charge for the damage to my uniform and for two evenings I had to report to the guardhouse in full kit, then stand outside in the freezing cold for two hours. It was quite a contrast from the early part of my life in Pretoria. Once again, just as on the Scandinavian trip, I was a quick learner and didn't do that again.

Since Padgate was something of a transit camp, there were new recruits arriving on a regular basis and there would soon be a familiar face among us. One of those that arrived shortly after me was Archie Glen, another footballer who played at wing-half for Aberdeen. We would become good friends and eventually face each other many times in matches between our respective clubs.

After our initial training we were allowed home for a long weekend, but on my return I was told that I was being transferred and had to report to another camp – the RAF School of Fire Fighting and Rescue at Sutton-on-Hull.

It was quite ironic that I was sent to the firefighting school after burning my trousers. The camp at Sutton was similar to Padgate in that it was on the fringes of the town, but other than being in quite pleasant countryside, there was not a lot to do. I remained at Sutton-on-Hull for a six-week stint during which time I followed the aerodrome fireman course. Some of the conscripts fancied an overseas tour with combat, but there would be no action for me in the RAF, other than what I could find on the football field. Unfortunately, however, it did not seem that there would be much prospect of any football at Padgate or, initially, at Hull, unless I managed to get back to Glasgow.

If life in the RAF through National Service in these two camps was a little tedious, it was certainly good for instilling some regimented discipline among the lower ranks. The day began at 5.30am when we would get up, although reveille was at 6am. Everything had to be tidied, uniform pressed and boots cleaned in time for breakfast at 6.45am. I had no bother adapting to this life in the RAF, but I was desperate to resume my football at Rangers. I realised that to get back into the frame and the team, I would have to wait for the odd break home for the chance to play. In reality, I would have to forget about first-team football for almost the rest of the 1951/52 season as the RAF was restrictive to my movement through much of that early period. As a consequence, any time I did manage to get back that season, I had to make do with life in the reserves.

The Commanding Officer was generally sympathetic to my position and after my first week at Hull, he let me return home to play in the semi-final of the Reserve Cup. If it was a sign of compassion for my football career, he did not follow it up the following week when we were scheduled to play Aberdeen in the final. I was keen to get away to play in the game and I asked for permission to leave the camp, but he refused. Indeed, it seemed that I would not be due leave for a further four weeks and would be stuck at the camp. It was at times like these I felt quite isolated from things back at Ibrox, especially when there were important games coming up. I was determined to play in the final, but that could not happen if I was not granted my leave papers. Without the permission of the CO and quite undeterred by my restriction to the camp, I decided to go AWOL – Absent Without Leave. It was a seriously big decision and I knew that it was one that could have grave consequences if I was caught.

After duty on the Friday evening, I jumped the fence with my kitbag and walked towards the station. On the way, I met a young pilot officer who was heading for the train back home to Aberdeen. As I was walking with him and explaining what I had done, he was alarmed that I had jumped camp and said, 'Don't walk with me – I'll see

143

you on the train!' He did not want to be seen with me in case I was caught and he was seen to be an 'accomplice'. I let him go on and I headed to the station on my own. I managed to catch the train before the camp even knew I had gone and I was soon on my way back up the track to Scotland.

I played in the match and we beat Aberdeen 2-0, so all the trouble I faced in getting there was worthwhile and it gave me a good chance to catch up with my friends back at Ibrox again. I stayed over until the Sunday, but later that night I headed back south, arriving in Hull at 5am on the Monday. A few of the others who had managed to get passes for the weekend were also at the station and there were some taxis waiting to take us back to the camp. All of the boys knew by this time what I had done and they helped me to sneak back in. There were times when being small was a distinct advantage – and this was one of them. As I approached the guardhouse, I ducked among them and went through without being noticed. I had got away with it! Nobody had missed me, although if I had been caught, it would have been another charge.

Through my first year on National Service, the football season of 1951/52 had not been a good one for Rangers. The club lost out in the championship once again to Hibernian and to Motherwell at the quarter-final stage of the Scottish Cup. Rangers did reach the final of the League Cup but lost narrowly to Dundee who scored a last-minute goal for a 3-2 win. There was great disappointment around Ibrox at another poor season and I was also frustrated that I had hardly figured. As the season neared its conclusion, I did finally get a chance to play in the first team once again, when injury to Willie Waddell and Willie Thornton left the team short-handed in attack. I was drafted in for a match against Partick Thistle in the first round of the Glasgow Charity Cup. Colin Liddell, who had taken the outside-left position throughout, was switched to the inside. I had a good match in a 4-3 win for Rangers and I retained my place for the semi-final against Third Lanark, but we lost the game 1-0.

Another barren season had ended and I had not played any meaningful part. When I first came to Ibrox, I had been impatient for a chance to show what I could do in the first team. Mr Struth gave me my chance against Partick Thistle, but I soon knew that I would have to serve my apprenticeship before I could expect a regular run. More importantly, I had to show the Boss that I deserved a run in the side. The two seasons of 1950/51 and 1951/52 had been very disappointing for the club and frustrating for me. I knew that I would have to break through soon if I was to make it at Ibrox, although I still had the complication of National Service. There was little I could do other than to continue to train as well as I could, try to get weekend passes, and seize the chance when it came around. The start of the 1952/53 season marked my third year in Scotland and I wanted it to be my year. Whether it would be Rangers' year too, remained to be seen.

The club got off to the worst possible start in the new season with a 5-0 defeat to Hearts in the opening match of the League Cup sectional matches. Colin Liddell had retained his place in the outside-left position, while I was confined to the reserves once again. Although the club recovered from that reverse to go on to win the section, they lost the first Old Firm match of the season at Parkhead in the middle of September.

Although Liddell scored Rangers' only goal in the 2-1 defeat, the press were speculating about whether Rangers would make a change on the left wing again. Clearly Liddell was not impressing.

I was re-introduced to the side in a league match against Third Lanark immediately following the Celtic game – the only change in the side, with Colin Liddell stepping to the sidelines. We won 4-1 and I had a hand in a couple of the goals. Ironically, the margin could have been greater when we got a penalty near the end. Ian McColl decided to take it and his attempt was saved. I had just come back into the team, so I could hardly expect them to hand me the ball at the penalty, although by then I was the regular penalty taker in the reserves. There was no disappointment – just great pleasure that I had come back into the team and we had won convincingly.

We suffered a reverse in the Glasgow Cup Final, losing 3-1 to Partick Thistle, when I scored the only goal and for a few games the outside-left position was swapped between Liddell and me. However, from November I finally got the run that I had been looking for in the three years I had spent at Ibrox. The turning point came in a league match against Clyde at Shawfield. We won the match 6-4 and, although I did not get on the scoresheet, the correspondent in the *Evening Times* reported that I had a 'bright game'. It was a good contest for Billy Simpson too, who got a hat-trick and John Prentice who was now my inside-forward. Colin Liddell eventually drifted out of the picture and he eventually left Ibrox a couple of years later after playing only a fleeting few games.

The camp Commanding Officer at Hull had been very good in permitting me to leave to travel north each week to play for Rangers, although travelling to Glasgow was still limiting. Indeed, sometimes there were no opportunities to get back north to join up with the team. However, during the 1952/53 season, I was transferred from the camp at Hull to what would be my final station at RAF Warton, next to the village of Freckleton, near Lytham. Again I was assigned to the camp as an 'aerodrome fireman', which was quite funny because there was no aerodrome in the area where we were stationed. We had to tend some big hangars though and our routine would be in training with firefighting equipment. If Hull had been a little restrictive, things were a bit more relaxed at Warton and I managed to get more time off for my football. In fact, I was back home more or less every weekend, although, like Hull, getting back to Glasgow was not always straightforward.

By the time I had arrived at Warton, I had established myself in the first team and managed to work around my National Service commitments with the help of the senior officers at Hull. I expected that the same could be organised at Warton when I arrived there, so on the day of my arrival – a Friday – I had to get a pass to go home for the weekend. We had a big match coming up against Celtic so it was essential that I get the clearance to leave camp to travel north. I reported at 8am and by lunchtime I had completed all the necessary paperwork, met the rest of the crew and imagined that it would all be quite straightforward. I was entitled to the leave so I did not expect that there would be any problem. The procedures were generally quite routine – at least, that is what I thought. When I went to get the pass, I was shocked to find that the normal procedure at Warton was for all passes to be administered by the Thursday, so I was 24 hours too late. I was expected back in Glasgow to play, but without a pass it seemed there would be no chance. The officer-in-charge was very helpful and suggested that if I could return to camp by am on Monday, I would not be missed as the Flight Sergeant was a bit dopey.

I took that cue as some kind of endorsement to head home and travelled back to Glasgow. I played for Rangers on the Saturday and we won, then I returned nice and early on the Monday morning. I expected that I could slip into the camp as the officer-in-charge had suggested, but when I arrived, I was told by the boys that I was on a charge. The Flight Sergeant had discovered that I was AWOL after all, and he was far from happy. Apparently, on the Friday I had received three phonecalls from friends who wanted to wish me well ahead of the big game. Each had called looking to speak with me and pass on their best wishes, only to find that I was not at my station. They meant well, but when I was not around to take the calls, the Flight Sergeant was alerted that I was missing. He immediately set about a search of the camp, before he realised that I was on my way north. A charge was inevitable and when I returned, I was placed on duty in full kit for two hours for three successive nights after work.

Although I was not happy with my 'well-wishers' at the time, I did actually build up a great relationship with each of them from then onwards. They included

Pilot Fitness Officer Bob Crampsey, who became a distinguished journalist and broadcaster. Bob became famous as one of the presenters on STV's football programme, *Scotsport*, and he also wrote a column for the *Evening Times*. He was as keen on sport as I was and he was something of a soulmate with his love of both football and cricket. In football, he was a Queen's Park man and a bit of an authority on the club, although he had a wide knowledge of the game. He was also a decent goalkeeper in the RAF football team, although he never managed to play at a higher level. He was comfortable in anything football, but he was equally at home in the world of cricket. We both played in the cricket team, where he was the wicketkeeper. Bob became a great friend and we would go on to meet many times in the future.

Another of the 'well-wishers' was Bedding Store Officer Joe MacLean, who became a minister. When my daughter Linda was just a baby, he vowed that he would conduct her wedding ceremony when the time came. True to his word, he did officiate at her wedding in the Parkstone Hotel in Prestwick some time ago. The third of the well-wishers was the station Telephone Officer, David Cowan. David and Joe were to remain good friends of the family long after I had left the RAF.

After I did my time for this misdemeanour, things did get easier for me. I guess they realised that I could combine my duties at the camp, while travelling back to play for Rangers and the camp officers were very helpful in arranging things. The Chief Fire Officer told me that I had been given permission to get off every weekend to play for Rangers, which was a great concession, allowing me the chance to develop my career in football. The regular weekend releases did not affect my contribution to the RAF and, in any case, the boys at the camp were very helpful in covering for me while I was away. In gratitude, I used to bring them back tit-bits, such as cigarettes and football programmes. They were a great bunch of lads and were very supportive throughout my time in the RAF.

Although for both professional and personal reasons, I would have rather been at Ibrox and back home with the family, I was enjoying life in the RAF. There was good camaraderie and always great banter among the servicemen. Indeed, serving in the forces was not a chore at all. Sport was my life in South Africa and it had also become a big part of my life in the RAF too, away from our regular duties. In the winter I played football and in the summer I played cricket and tennis regularly. I also took part in athletics and was asked by the fire officer to run for the station in the Inter Station Athletics Championships. The senior officers had been good to me over the winter and I felt that I could not refuse. I was to compete in both the 880 metres and also the mile, neither of which I had great experience in. I was not concerned, because I was fit – or at least I thought I was. I ran in the pre-qualifying and reached the final of the 880 metres, which was scheduled to follow the mile the next day. However, in the morning, I was so stiff that I had to withdraw from the mile so that I could compete in the 880 final. I finished fourth and could not walk for a week.

Football in the armed forces for professional players necessitated a balance between club commitments and responsibilities to the camp. We generally played the services matches in midweek, which allowed time for the professional players to play for their teams at the weekend. As a result of the distance between the camp and Glasgow, it was a strange period for me serving in the camp in England midweek and travelling back to Scotland every weekend to play for Rangers. However, I was not the only sportsman on National Service and Rangers was not the only team I played for in the period. I also played with the RAF team and what a formidable side that was! It included many professional players who had also been assigned to the RAF at the time and among them were South African international Eddie Firmani (Charlton), Scotland's Jackie Moodie (Blackpool), Welshman John Charles and England internationals Ray Woods (Manchester United), Malcolm Finlayson (Wolves), Peter Sillett (Chelsea), Peter Broadbent and Ron Flowers (both Wolves).

When I played with the RAF team, we had matches against the other service teams, as well as the likes of Oxford University. The culmination of our matches against the other divisions of the armed forces came at the end of March 1953, when we defeated the Army team – giving us the title for the first time in a number of years. With such top-quality players in our ranks, the standard in the matches involving the forces was very high and football between the different services was considered very important to morale. The matches against the other forces were always very competitive, but they did not have anything to compare in the edge to one game we played while I was in the RAF. It was an 'international' clash that had been arranged in Belgrade, behind the Iron Curtain, with the Red Star Army team. They had seven Yugoslavian internationals in their side and they beat us 7-4, but the game was tagged as one of the best seen in Belgrade.

With so much at stake in national pride and prestige, there was always a risk of injury playing in these matches. However there was no question that I had to represent the RAF, especially in such an important game. The match was very physical and I sustained a bad muscle injury, which was not helped by the trip home to Glasgow on the Thursday. I had a severe limp and by the Friday, it was no better. On the Saturday I could walk, although I was still in some pain. When I turned up at Ibrox, I expected to be listed to play against East Fife and I was a little sceptical that I could play. I did not want to admit that I had been injured in the RAF match, especially since I was trying to get back into the side. Sure enough, my name was on the team list and I reckoned that I might be able to run it off. We won that game and I played one of my best ever games for Rangers, even though I probably should not have been on the pitch.

Being away from Glasgow, I missed Rangers, but not more than Ella and our new baby Linda. Warton was going to be my last camp so I decided to move the family down to England. I had settled down in the area and we rented a house in Freckleton, which was ideal for us. We were very happy down there, and if I was not on duty in the camp or spending time with Ella and Linda, I played cricket and tennis. It was a nice opportunity to live away from Glasgow in another area for a time, despite the difficulties it presented to my football career. Eventually we would leave to head home, of course, but in Freckleton I had the best of both worlds. I could serve out my time with the RAF and enjoy life with my young family in a nice area.

Having now secured my place in the team and settled with the family in a nice village near the camp, I was completely comfortable with life. At Ibrox, things were looking better for the club too. Although Rangers had made a slow start in the 1952/53 season, we had managed to get a run of victories, losing just once between the end of October and the middle of March. That put the club in a strong position in the league and we were also going well in the Scottish Cup. We followed up victory over Celtic in the quarter-finals by beating Hearts in the semi-finals, as a place against Aberdeen in the final beckoned. Meanwhile, our main title contenders Hibernian had completed their campaign by the end of April, leaving us three points adrift with two games in hand. At that time, two points were awarded for a win, not three as nowadays. The league was important to us but the premier competition was the Scottish Cup and I was desperate to win my first major cup medal.

We warmed up for the final with a match at Fir Park, where we comfortably defeated Motherwell 3-0. We thought it would send something of a psychological message to Aberdeen, who lost 4-1 to the Steelmen two days earlier. We were very much mistaken! The day before the match, Aberdeen travelled to Gleneagles Hotel and made their preparations there and while the rest of the Rangers squad went to Turnberry, I travelled up from Lancashire, by train. Aberdeen went into the match free from injury, but we had some personnel changes to contend with. Our regular centre-half,

Willie Woodburn, was suspended and Sammy Cox was on the sidelines with an injury sustained in the Home International match against England at Wembley a week earlier. Mr Struth selected Duncan Stanners in the middle of the defence to replace Woodburn and Jim Pryde took Sammy Cox's place. More importantly to me, I was selected on the left wing.

When the Saturday came, the headlines proclaimed the Knighthood of Sir Winston Churchill in a ceremony that the Queen performed at Windsor the night before. It was perhaps an omen, because there was coincidence in that he had visited Ibrox in May 1949, just a few weeks before I first arrived at the stadium. I hoped that there would be a recurrence of coincidence as he celebrated a great moment in his life, while I did likewise in my career. The newspapers paid their own tribute to a famous politician and wartime hero on the hearing of the honour conferred upon him. However, I had my eyes set on a quite different honour – a Scottish Cup winner's medal.

We arrived at Hampden resplendent in our new blazers with the bright new Rangers crest on the pocket. We felt very proud as we entered the stadium with the noise of the welcoming fans ringing in our ears. If it was a big match for me, it was also very special for George Young. He had played in many big matches for Rangers and already had three Scottish Cup medals, but this was to be his first final as team captain. He strode forward confidently towards the halfway line, completed the formalities and then won the toss of the coin in the centre circle. He elected to play with the traditional Rangers end behind us, playing towards the east terracing – the traditional 'away' end. In his previous cup finals, 'Corky' had played under Jock Shaw's captaincy. This time Jock sat in the stand, firmly behind us, but with his interest probably a little divided. At left-back for Aberdeen was his brother, Davie Shaw. Just a few years earlier they had the unique distinction of facing each other in a major cup final – the Victory Cup – Davie for Hibs and Jock with Rangers.

When the match kicked off in front of 129,762 fans, we were overwhelming favourites, but football can have its twists and turns and we never took anything for granted. Things looked good for us in the early stages of the match and with just eight minutes on the clock I stroked a pass inside Aberdeen's full-back and through to John Prentice. He played the ball quickly, shooting towards the far post, which sent the Dons keeper Martin scrambling across his goal. To the keeper's surprise, the ball drifted across him and tucked into the corner of the net. It was the perfect start and I remember the Rangers fans in full voice.

Aberdeen were a proud side, however, and came roaring back at us. After a few near-misses the game was turned upside down in the 27th minute with a bad injury to our keeper George Niven. He was caught as he dived at the feet of the Aberdeen centre-forward Paddy Buckley who was careering in on goal. Niven was badly injured and as we gathered around him, it seemed that he would be unable to continue. He was stretchered from the field and, with no substitutes allowable at that time in football, we had to select a deputy. Big Corky stepped forward defiantly and took the goalkeeper's yellow jersey, hauling it over his blue one. It looked like we would be left to see out the match with ten men and with our captain, an outfield player, between the posts. The defence which had already been makeshift with the absence of Woodburn and Cox was now totally reorganised. Willie Waddell went into Corky's right-back position and we played with just four forwards.

For the rest of the half it was very much a case of backs to the wall as Aberdeen seized the initiative, battering our goal from every angle. We stood firm and Corky performed admirably as we kicked balls off the line and fought to keep our lead intact. For me, it was more a case of trying to make tackles and hold the ball, rather than attacking constantly.

When we got into the dressing room with our slender one-goal lead, our first concern was Niven. His head was bandaged and he had received stitches to his ear. However, he was declared fit enough to go back out, although hardly ready for a game of football, let alone a cup final. Our trainer Jimmy Smith sat behind our goal ready to attend to him if he should break down again as the second half commenced.

Outfield, we could not break the Aberdeen momen-tum, but it looked like we might hold on, until the Dons managed to grasp the equaliser with a header from Yorston with just ten minutes to go. From there, it looked like Aberdeen would go on to win, but we held out and the match went to a replay. We knew that we had not given a good account of ourselves and, although I had played reasonably well and laid on the goal, we all saw the replay as a chance to redeem ourselves. I think if we had not had to contend with the injury to Niven, we would have won the game outright, but the alterations to the team certainly caused some disruption to our plans and performance.

The replay took place again at Hampden, just four days later on 29 April 1953, and again a huge crowd gathered to watch the sides. The official attendance was 113,700, meaning that over 243,000 fans had taken in the two matches of the final. The newspapers said that around 23,000 had travelled south with Aberdeen for the first match, so that would mean that we probably had at least 90,000 and maybe nearer 100,000 of our own fans inside Hampden on the Saturday. With fewer Dons fans travelling on the Wednesday for the replay, our contingent must have been around the same again. Who knows how many neutrals were there, but it was clear that most inside the ground were in blue as I looked around the terraces.

We went into the game with Willie Woodburn, fresh from suspension, cleared to play, as Duncan Stanners stood aside. John Prentice also made way for Billy Simpson who came in to lead the line. Despite these changes, the replay settled into the same pattern as the first game and we were under the cosh for the first 20 minutes or so. Our defence remained resolute as Aberdeen looked to be increasingly frustrated. As the first half progressed, we gained more of a grip on the game and I found more space. Our breakthrough came with just four minutes left until the half-time break. I linked up with Derek Grierson and Willie Paton, to slide the ball through to Billy Simpson and he did what he always did best – striking the ball low into the right-hand corner of the net. The Aberdeen players were crestfallen, because they had had the best of the match up to that

157

stage and should have been in the lead. However, matches are won on goals scored and we were 1-0 up as we went in at the interval.

In the second half, Ian McColl was in fine form, helping out in defence and making great probing runs into attack. Aberdeen did not trouble us as much in the second half and as the match neared a conclusion, we had opportunities to add to our scoring. When referee Jack Mowat blew his whistle at the end of the match, our joy was tinged with some relief. Aberdeen had played well in the two games and many felt they deserved more from the tie. For us, however, it sealed our 14th Scottish Cup win and the tenth for Mr Struth. More importantly for me, it was my first – and ultimately only – Scottish Cup medal. The win provided the first part of a possible domestic double and as we returned to the St Enoch Hotel to celebrate our victory, I had a feeling of huge satisfaction. With my medal tucked safely into my pocket, I was satisfied that I had achieved one of my goals. Just four years earlier I had joined Mr Struth for dinner on my arrival in Glasgow, as a young aspiring South African. Here in the same hotel where we dined that day, I celebrated a win for Rangers in the country's premier tournament and I was part of it all.

There were celebrations at Ibrox in the aftermath of our win, but we did not have long to dwell upon them. Our season was not over – we still had the league title very much in our sights. Reigning champions Hibernian had completed all of their matches and sat at the top of the table three points clear, but we had two games in hand. I travelled back south to the camp, but my stay was short as I headed north again just three days later for one of the two outstanding league matches – against Dundee at Ibrox. A win and a draw would be enough to give us the title, but only if we could overtake Hibs' better goal average. If we scored three goals against Dundee it would be enough to better the Easter Road side's average, leaving us needing just a draw at Queen of the South's Palmerston Park to win the championship. To the delight of the fans we won 3-1, getting both the victory and the goals. There was a bit of a carnival atmosphere at half-time when the Scottish Cup was paraded around Ibrox, while the Govan Silver Band played some Rangers songs. It was something of a tradition for the band to play at our matches.

With Dundee overcome, only a draw now stood between us and the championship – and a wonderful domestic double. As we revelled in anticipation, another winger was catching the headlines in England. Stanley Matthews helped his Blackpool side to a 4-3 win over Bolton Wanderers at Wembley in the FA Cup Final, in what would later be known as the 'Matthews Final'. His medal could not have meant more to him than mine did to me. I had the chance to add a league winner's medal though and we would travel to Dumfries five days later in pursuit of the final piece of silverware and glory. Before then, we were frustrated in losing a Charity Cup semi-final to Queen's Park, on the toss of a coin. It was hardly ideal preparation for a match that set up the chance of a title win. In fact, the Queen of the South match would be my tenth game in just five weeks, all played between trips to and from Freckleton.

The re-arrangements of the fixtures scheduled the Queen of the South match for a Thursday evening, which created a strange atmosphere for such a vital match. There were 17,000 fans inside Palmerston as we contested a gritty game against the Borders side. We were shocked just before half-time when Queens took the lead. We needed a draw at least, and in the second half we fought for the goal that could secure the title for us. With just 15 minutes left, Willie Waddell slammed the ball into the net to our great relief and the delight of our travelling support. It was all we needed as the match ended 1-1 and we were crowned First Division champions. In my first full season I had won a league and cup double and felt that I had really arrived. The world was my oyster, it seemed.

By now, I was nearing the end of my time in the RAF and my focus would be fully upon Rangers. When we started planning the return home, we encountered one major problem – having uprooted to live in Freckleton, we had no home to go to in Glasgow. We spent a bit of time looking around for a nice place to carry on the next stage of our life and we bought a semi-detached house in Stepps, just outside Glasgow for £1,800. Around the same time, a new RAF airman, Dennis Boyd, arrived at the camp. Dennis was a painter and decorator to trade and fortunately for me, football-daft. We got on famously and I told him about my new house and the work I had to do in it.

We reached a great deal – Dennis offered to help me out by painting my new house and during his stay I got him along to watch two of our games, one at Ibrox and the other away to Dundee. He did a grand job on the house and I am sure he enjoyed his little experience of Rangers.

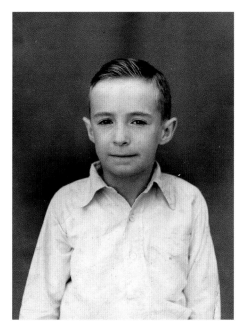

Johnny – Aged 7.

At Pretoria Zoo – Johnny (left), Daisy and Raymond, with Martha.

My Family – (l to r) Raymond, Johnny, Ruth, Mom, Daisy, and Dorothy.

Above, left: Family in uniform! Daisy in her flying gear, Raymond in his Naval Reserve uniform and me stripped for rugby!

Above, right: Mom in the front garden at our home in Tulleken Street, Pretoria.

Anyone for tennis…or cricket?

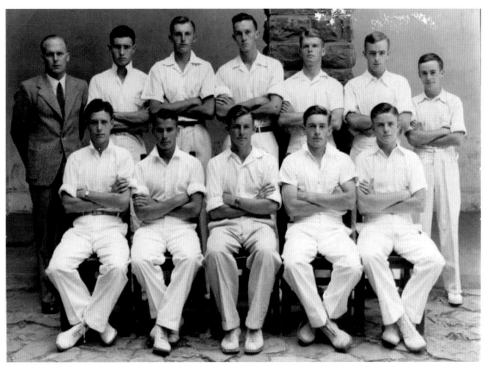

Pretoria High School First XI Cricket team. I am back right.

Pretoria High School Tennis team. I am on the left.

DAILY RECORD   EVENING NEWS   SUNDAY MAIL

KEMSLEY HOUSE, GLASGOW. C.2

(TELEPHONE: CITy 7000)   7th June, 1949.

Dear Alec,

      I have been in touch with Bill Struth, and he says he shall be delighted to give Hubbard a chance of playing for Rangers. Keep it under your hat, as I want the scoop of it.

      Rangers will pay his passage here, and in the words of Bill Struth, "The boy will be well looked after while he is with us." If he makes the grade, he will, of course, be well paid by the Rangers, but if he fails to come up to their standard, they will see to it that he has his passage paid back to South Africa.

      I think your first step should be to get Hubbard, or yourself, to write immediately to Director-Manager Struth, mentioning what I have told you, and awaiting developments. Let me know how it goes.

      In a hurry,

                              All the best,

                              Willie Allison

                              Sports Editor.

A.L. Prior, Esq.,
26 George Street,
Rosettenville,
Johannesburg,
SOUTH AFRICA.

My letter from Willie Allison, arranging my 'trial' with Rangers.

Farewells from Mom (left), Dorothy (centre) and Daisy (right) at Jan Smutts Airport, Pretoria – 17th July 1949.

A walk around Ibrox Park on my first day at Rangers Football Club.

Signing for Rangers watched by the legendary manager Bill Struth.

Flyweight boxer visits Russell Moreland's shop in Glasgow. Moreland is centre and I am left.

Some of the old guard with Mr Struth at Sammy Cox's wedding. (l to r) Cox, Bill Struth, Torry Gillick and Willie Thornton.

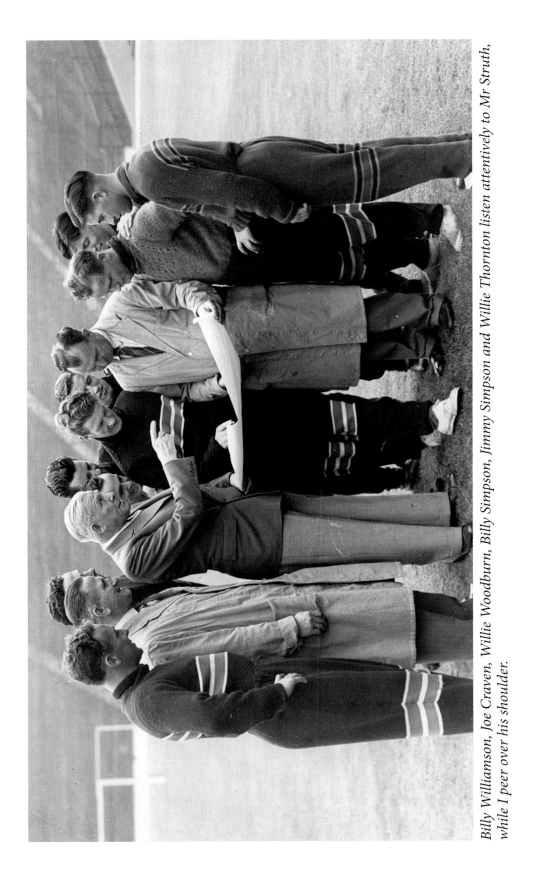

Billy Williamson, Joe Craven, Willie Woodburn, Billy Simpson, Jimmy Simpson and Willie Thornton listen attentively to Mr Struth, while I peer over his shoulder.

Ella, Mom and me.

In my RAF uniform with daughter Linda at Blackpool.

Training at Ibrox with Ian McColl (left), Ralph Brand (centre), and Alex Scott (right).

Left to Right: Willie McCulloch, Derek Grierson, Billy Simpson, John Prentice, me.

Family bliss - Ella with newborn John, Raymond and Linda.

The Scottish League team.

The players stand on the edge of the area anticipating a goal – the perfect penalty!

South African pals: Ken Hewkins and Don Kichenbrand (rear) with Syd O'Linn and me at the front, before the Scotland–South Africa match.

The Scotland Cap!

The 1953 Scottish League champions and Scottish Cup winners – the domestic double! I am back row far right.

A Bury team group.

In action with Rangers.

Warming up with Bury.

Proudly receiving my MBE.

Inducted into the Rangers 'Hall of Fame'.

When my time in the RAF ended, I had some mixed feelings as we packed up to return home to Glasgow. We were delighted to return home, but we had such an enjoyable time in Lancashire and met good friends, that it was something of a wrench. I would not have chosen to go into National Service and there is no doubt that it did disrupt my career, despite me doing everything to work the system and get back at weekends to play. However, I look back upon these two wonderful years in the RAF with great affection. I met some great characters and wonderful friends through that short period – many of whom remained great friends for a considerable time. I feel that the discipline of National Service made me a stronger, more respectful character. I have no doubts that this is what Mr Struth liked about the services and I was certainly better for it. I have always been a quick learner and it did not take me long to understand how important discipline and respect were to the services and everyday life. I also learned to enjoy the camaraderie with the others and when you join the services, everyone is essentially in the same boat. I was a professional football player, but we were all equals and I was regarded as just one of the boys. It was a good part of my education in life and I thoroughly enjoyed it. Life in the RAF was good and there were lots of laughs.

Even today, some time after I left Warton to return home, I look back upon that period extremely fondly. Life in the services probably limited my appearances for Rangers in the beginning, but I am eternally grateful for the efforts of the senior officers in arranging things to allow me to play for Rangers. My appearances were curtailed, but the opportunity to return frequently provided me with the chance to maintain my place within the team at a critical stage in my career. By the time I left the services, I was well established in the side at Rangers. I felt proud that I had done my stint in National Service and now I could concentrate on my career – as a first-11 Rangers player.

10

Goodbye
Mr Struth – Hello
Mr Symon

WITH National Service behind me and my place in the first team secure, life was good. Early in 1954 we had an addition to the family when our first son, Raymond, was born. Like Linda, he was delivered at Stobhill Hospital in Glasgow. We were by now settled in our new home in Stepps with very good neighbours around us. My family were back in South Africa, but I was now completely immersed in my wife's family in Scotland. Ella had two brothers, Alex and Colin and one sister, Josie. Like me, Ella was the baby of the family. We saw all of her family regularly and Gran Black (Ella's mum) came to stay with us, playing a big part in our household. She was good company for Ella when I was away and helped in the burdens of raising the kids. On matchdays, Ella and Josie were regulars at the football, while gran did the babysitting. When we all came home after the game, she would also have tea ready. It was a blissful domestic situation and I could not have been happier.

While it was good to be back in Glasgow after life in the services, I found the transition to full-time football strange. Once again I had time to spare and instead of the regular midweek games in the RAF allied to my Rangers duties, I had just one match most weeks at Ibrox. To help fill in the time, I picked up the snooker cue again and entered the West of Scotland Snooker Championships. I did not make many headlines and exited at the first-round stage, but the West Nile Street hall was one of my haunts and I still went down whenever I could.

Back at Ibrox, things were not going too well for the team and Mr Struth was ailing. His health had become increasingly a concern and his influence started to wane. The team that had done so well in the previous season seemed to lose some of its sparkle as key players moved into the latter stages of their careers. Results were not going our way and there was a growing unrest among the fans. Having been the predominant team through the 1940s and continuing that success with the double in 1953, they found it hard to deal with a team that was languishing deep in the First Division. Even Mr Struth himself came in for some veiled criticism and in a letter to the press, one fan spoke in almost derogatory terms of the 'grand old man'.

The pivotal result came in the middle of April, when we lost heavily to Aberdeen (6-0) in the Scottish Cup semi-final. By then we had also virtually given up on the title in that 1953/54 season.

I believe that Mr Struth had originally intended to leave at the end of the season, but after the Aberdeen defeat, I think he decided to move sooner. In reality, our poor form was probably attributable to a lack of consistency in team selection through injury or players moving on. It seemed that all season, we had struggled to get the same 11 on the field and in a few games some players went out half-fit. In many ways the team had reached a transitional stage, with the manager aware that he needed to freshen things up. However, he was an old man by this stage and his poor health must have been limiting on his ability to rebuild the side.

It was clear that the directors were feeling the pressure and in the match after the Aberdeen defeat, they issued a statement in the match programme. It read, 'We shall go forward grimly determined to restore this famous old club to the position it must hold in the world of soccer. That is our duty; none will shirk from it come what may. Evidence will soon be forthcoming. We cannot at the moment reveal our plans but the supporters will be informed once the results of our discussions have become known.'

It could only have meant that the club was planning some changes in personnel, but we did not quite expect the news that was to emerge at the end of the month. It was then that Mr Struth caused something of a shock by formally resigning his position as manager of Rangers Football Club. It was very much the end of an era for Rangers as he had been at the club for 40 years. The announcement came just before we were due to play

Celtic in a first-round tie in the Glasgow Charity Cup at Ibrox. By then, the league championship had gone to our Old Firm rivals and we had lost out in the two major cup competitions. The Charity Cup was the only piece of silverware available to us, but it was scant compensation in a difficult season.

With the news of Struth's departure resonating around Hampden, we defeated Celtic 1-0 to knock them out of the tournament. However, even that trophy eluded us as Third Lanark went on to take the honours by beating us in the final. Mr Struth did not attend that last Old Firm match as he was not well enough. A few days later, we presented him with a farewell gift of a TV radiogram in the Blue Room at Ibrox. It was perhaps a small gesture, but it did not fully convey our thoughts and gratitude. I was very sad to see him leave and, like all of the other players, I owed him a huge debt for giving me the opportunity to play with this great club.

The 1953/54 campaign had ended in great disappointment, but we were not quite ready to close the curtain on football that season. We dusted ourselves down and headed off on the liner *Empress of Scotland* for a tour of North America. Disappointedly, Mr Struth did not join the party – his days of travelling with the club well behind him. For the rest of us, it was a welcome break, although it was shaping up to be a hectic one. Over the three weeks of the tour we played eight matches across Canada and the USA. We were also scheduled to play three games against Chelsea, each taking place in different cities – Montreal, Toronto and New York – as well as a number of local matches in Hamilton, Winnipeg, Vancouver and Vancouver Island.

As if to confirm my place as a first-team regular, I was selected to play in seven of the eight games of the tour. I was delighted to be involved in so many of the matches but after such a long hard season, the travelling was onerous, although enjoyable. The regular matches across the continent aside, the tour was to have some special significance to me, marking an important milestone in my career. It was on this trip that I took my first penalty for Rangers. Ironically, out first goal of the tour had come from a penalty, but courtesy of big Corky. That gave us a one-goal win over Chelsea in Montreal and a nice opening to the tour. We followed that up with a 6-0 win against a select side called Hamilton All Stars and then a 4-1 win against the Ontario All Stars. By then, the games – and the victories – were coming thick and fast. We then played British Columbia Mainland All Stars, which was a select side of the best that Canada could muster.

It was in this game that I was given the opportunity to take that first penalty. Until then, I had to stand by and watch as the ball was picked up by others whenever a penalty was awarded. Through most of the early part of my career the kicks would be taken by either Willie Waddell or George Young, both somewhat seasoned experts from the penalty spot, although they also missed their fair share. As a youngster just breaking into the team, I had no problem with that as they were experienced players. They had been generally making a decent effort of them, so I was quite content to let them get on with it. Even when a young Eric Caldow broke through, he got a chance to take a few penalties, but they never came my way. In the early stages of my career I never really pushed for the role, concentrating more on my overall performance.

Things changed for me in that match against British Columbia. We were well on top and, during the game, Corky came over to me and said, 'If we get a penalty today, the job's yours.' He had watched me take the kicks at training and he knew that I had a 100 per cent record in the reserves. So, as we piled the pressure on the Canadian defence and the goals began to flow, there came the moment when I would have the chance to step forward into the limelight. A foul inside the box on one of our forwards saw the referee point to the spot. I looked across at Corky and he nodded, 'It's yours.' I stepped forward and picked up the ball, placing it carefully on the spot.

It was a routine I was well familiar with, so I had no nerves. Composed, I walked back a few paces, then running straight on to the ball, I struck it firmly and comfortably into the right of the goal. The goalkeeper did not get near it. I had laid down a marker for the future. Who knows what would have happened if I had missed that kick? Would the responsibility have passed to someone else with my chance gone?

It is immaterial, because I did score from the spot and it would not be the last time. I actually scored two goals that day, including that crucial penalty and we won the match at a canter, 9-0. The scoreline could have been even greater if it was not for some biased refereeing. Just before time, he disallowed a goal by blowing his whistle while the ball was in flight and on its way into the net. Despite our dominance of the game, one of the local Vancouver pressmen decided to have a go at us after the match, saying we were a poor side and unsporting. I have noticed that recent managers at Ibrox have used the noticeboard in the home changing room to motivate the team or specific players. This was no different. We were annoyed at the press comments, which only served to fire us up for the remainder of the tour.

The North American tour had been a good one for me. Apart from that first penalty that would establish me as the club's regular penalty taker from then on, I had played well throughout and scored six goals. When the tour was complete, the record books showed that we had remained undefeated against Canadian opposition in Canada, but lost out to Chelsea in the penultimate game of the tour in Toronto. In our final game of the three matches against them, we drew 0-0, and having beaten them in that first match of the tour, the honours were even.

It was a great three weeks for the team in North America, but besides us coming to terms with the end of Mr Struth's reign it signalled the end of an era for two of the best players to have represented the club – Jock 'Tiger' Shaw (better known to his team-mates as 'Bas') and Willie Thornton. Both decided to hang up their boots at the end of the tour. They had joined Rangers in the mid-1930s and had become household names. Jock Shaw was one of the great characters in the club and even after he hung up his boots, he continued to work at Ibrox, as groundsman, for a long time after his playing career finished. I only played with him for a short period, but in his time he had been a great Rangers captain and although he was small, he was stocky and very formidable. You could say he was another good little 'un! I always found him to be a friendly chap and a good team-mate.

Willie Thornton had been interviewed by Dundee for the vacant manager's position just before we left on the tour and had agreed to join them on his return. He signed off from Rangers in the final game, against Chelsea, when he came on as substitute. His departure was another sign of the transition the team was undergoing as new and younger players emerged to become regulars. One of these young stars of the future, who joined us on the tour was full-back Eric Caldow, who came from Cumnock. He had come into the team earlier in the season, but this was his first tour and he settled in very well. He would become a great Rangers player in the future.

When I returned from the tour, the close season started for us and I took the opportunity to spend more time with the family, going away on holiday for a spell. Within a couple of weeks, Rangers announced the replacement for Mr Struth. His name was Scot Symon. For the club, it seemed that the new man would offer some continuity to the role that Mr Struth had created in a tenure of 34 years in the manager's office. Symon had played under Struth through the 1930s and 40s and obviously knew the club well. He had also served a valuable apprenticeship as a manager and seemed to show some talent in this regard. When he left Rangers he had gone on to become manager at East Fife and then Preston North End, earning many plaudits. Mr Struth was also impressed by Symon and had suggested his appointment to the board. For all his early success as a manager, I did not really know him at that time, but his appointment at Rangers was expected to continue the good work of Mr Struth in what was expected to be a seamless transition. On the face of it, there seemed every reason to expect Mr Symon to ease into the role that Struth had created, but for me, any optimism that Symon would be a younger version of Mr Struth was dashed very early in his time at Rangers. I was to find that Mr Symon was no Mr Struth.

While I did not know, or even hear, of Mr Struth when I first joined the club back in 1949, I quickly learned that Rangers revolved around him. I knew that he was not a football player himself, having come from an athletics background, but he was in complete control at Ibrox.

Like most managers of that era, he did not indulge in the tactical side of the game, but he was a wonderful manager of men. He epitomised everything that was good about Rangers and was my guiding hand through the five years I had been at the club. In many ways he was a father figure to me, but then again he was like that with everyone, from the jack-the-lad types like Torry Gillick, to the quieter players like Willie Waddell.

He never had any favourites and, although we all knew our place, he commanded our greatest respect. He cared for all of the players individually and would assist with advice and assistance even in personal matters. His authority was never in question and we knew where the line that should not be crossed was drawn. We all realised that he had great standing in the game and his record itself earned respect, but there was more to him than that. Above all, he was a nice man. There is no doubt that I would not have achieved all that I did at

Ibrox without him and I am eternally grateful for all of his guidance and help.

I have often reflected that I could have arrived from South Africa and left after just three months, but he had such confidence in me that he gave me that extended contract. As a youngster I was impatient for my chance to show what I could do and he realised my frustrations. He could have disregarded them, but he gave me that early experience in the first team, all the time ensuring that I would be pitched in against an opponent who would play me fairly. This was typical of his caring nature and the personal attention he devoted to his players. He earned our utmost respect and we knew him as 'the Boss', but affectionately so. When he decided to retire, we were all conscious that he had aged and that his health had become increasingly a problem. We knew that nothing is forever, so we bade him farewell and welcomed the new man with enthusiasm. Some of the older players knew Scot Symon particularly well, as they had played with him, but for the younger ones, including myself, it was a step into the unknown. I was not concerned, because the arrival of a new manager would not change my approach to training or to games. I always worked hard on the training field and would continue to do so. Having broken through into the first team, I did not intend to surrender my position easily and would work to impress the new boss.

When Symon arrived, we went through the formalities of our introductions then set about our normal routine at training. Within a short time, I could see some similarities in his approach to that adopted by Mr Struth, particularly with regard to the everyday things. Joe Craven and Jimmy Smith continued to take the training and, although like his predecessor, Symon did not get involved, he would generally stand trackside watching us go through the routines. We expected that there would be some changes, but in the beginning it seemed that life at Rangers under Symon would be very much the same as we had experienced under Mr Struth.

One of the first problems that Symon had to confront was the loss of key players such as Willie Thornton and Jock Shaw, so it was no surprise when he started to look around to add to his squad. We played our annual trial match on 9 August 1954 and, that day, there were 29 players on display who each got a chance to show the new manager what they could do. Five years earlier when I first joined the club and played in the same trial match, I was chosen for the Stripes to play against the Blues. This time, I was in the Blues, or first team, facing the Stripes. The Blues team that night was Niven, Young and Cox; Neillands, Woodburn and Rae; Waddell, Grierson, Simpson, Prentice, and me. The Stripes team was very experienced and included Brown, Caldow and Little; McKenzie, Stanners and Pryde; McCulloch, Paton, Gardiner, Findlay and Liddell.

The game finished all square at 1-1, but it gave us some idea as to how Symon might set up his team for the coming 1954/55 season. The forward line was relatively young with the exception of Waddell and the team was built upon an experienced back line with Young, Cox and Woodburn, the elder and more experienced statesmen. Sure enough, in our first match of the season, against Stirling Albion, only Sammy Cox (who got injured in the trial) and Ian Neillands were left out, as Ian McColl and Johnny Little came in to replace them. We got off to a flying start, winning 5-0. It seemed that Symon had worked wonders for the team and the plaudits he received after the match were generous. The one concern – and it was a big one – was the dismissal of Willie Woodburn, the fifth of his career.

The man we called 'Big Ben' had been sent off for the first time in August 1948, a year before I arrived at Ibrox. On that occasion he had been involved in a clash with the Motherwell centre-forward Davie Mathie and ended up with a two-week suspension. He remained clear of any further controversy for five years until March 1953, when he was involved in a rumpus with Clyde's Billy McPhail, who was the brother of Celtic's John McPhail. I played in that match and felt that Ben was reckless and probably deserved that second dismissal. He was banned for 21 days, but only six months later he was sent off against Stirling Albion and landed himself a six-week ban. Again, I was in the side that day. Ominously, the SFA warned him that it would view any further incidents seriously. Ironically, these two incidents were fairly tame in comparison to what turned out to be a final sending off and the pivotal moment in Woodburn's career in that match against Stirling Albion on 28 August 1954.

During the game, everything seemed fine with no aggravation and we were coasting at five goals ahead. I had managed to score myself and it seemed that we just had to play the game out for the perfect start to our season. Willie was carrying a knee injury and with just a minute to go, he clashed with Stirling's left-back Alec Paterson and the pair were left in a tangle on the floor. As he tried to get up when the ball broke clear, the Stirling player held his leg down and Willie reacted. Paterson punched him and Ben responded with a 'Glasgow Kiss'. The referee's official report gave the following, slightly different account, 'When the game was almost finished, Paterson, lying on the ground, caught Woodburn round the legs. As Paterson rose, Woodburn went towards him and struck him with his fist. When Woodburn was called to explain his actions to the SFA, he said that he had felt a jab of pain on his knee and lost his temper.'

In reality, the referee had no option but to send Ben off, but we knew that it could have a serious consequence to him. We never imagined it would be quite so draconian when they announced that he was suspended *sine die*, effectively ending his career. Although he had his moments on the pitch, he was a great player, and it was a disgrace that the SFA should take such a decision. When you see what happens in the modern game it seems quite harsh. He was a victim of his time, but even though the suspension was later rescinded, he was too old to play professionally.

The consequences were to leave Symon's preparations for the season in tatters as Woodburn was such an important player for us. He was the captain when I arrived and he was a great player who was well-respected by everyone. He was quite a gentleman, but was a very determined player and quick-tempered – even in friendly matches. He never liked to lose. I remember on our tour of Scandinavia in 1950, we played against Akademisk Boldklub and Bobby Brown lost a bizarre goal, when a long ball was played towards him. He let it bounce past him, assuming that it was going to slip past the post, but it crept in at the corner. Willie Woodburn ran half the length of the pitch to explain to our embarrassed goalkeeper that he was not happy!

On another occasion, we lost a match against Celtic and Willie came into the dressing room absolutely fuming. He took off his boot, slammed it on the floor and it bounced up, flying right over Mr Struth and straight through the window. On that occasion he got a stern ticking-off from the Boss and was told to report to him first thing Monday morning. Like all of these situations where some managerial discipline was administered, nobody ever found out what was said or what sanctions were imposed by Struth. Woodburn, like all players in this situation, never said anything either. It was the Rangers way of dealing with things.

Another incident with Woodburn took place at Starks Park, Kirkcaldy, when we slipped to a draw with Raith Rovers. In those days it was only a point dropped but it was a valuable one at a critical stage in the season. After the game we would have soft drinks and sometimes a bottle of lager. On this occasion, Willie picked up the bottle and, in a fit of anger, wrenched the top off. It exploded and splashed some of its contents over Mr Struth's suit. Once again Willie was summoned up the Marble Staircase and into the manager's office.

Training could be exciting with Ben too. On one occasion his competitive spirit was almost the undoing of John Little. John came in with a slide tackle that sent Woodburn crashing to the ground. Willie, who was the much bigger man, got up and squared up to John with fists ready for a fight. John raised his fists too and we expected a bit of a scrap, but Willie dropped his hands and walked away. Thankfully the red mist dissipated just as quickly as it had emerged and an ugly incident was averted. With such a competitive edge, it was inevitable that there would come times when Ben would clash with opponents and referees, but the sanction imposed by the SFA was unnecessary.

Woodburn is often remembered primarily for his troubles surrounding that *sine die* punishment, but he was a wonderful player for Rangers and Scotland. When Willie left in such unfortunate circumstances, ironically it gave a new lease of life to George Young. Corky had been a great right-back, but as he got older he had lost a bit of his speed. He moved from his right-back berth to the centre-half position, to replace Woodburn, and to my mind he then became a better player. By then he had learned to use his knowledge of the game to compensate for his lack of speed, reading opponents to make vital interceptions. He was a good captain and he also knew what to say and when to say it. On many occasions he would tell Willie Woodburn to take it easy when he started to lose his rag, although obviously that did not always work. However, he was a great character in the dressing room and became Mr Struth's leader on the field. He would now become Scot Symon's trusted captain as the new manager embarked on that first season of 1954/55 with his plans already disrupted by the loss of the influential Woodburn.

Having been at the club for five years and secured the outside-left position for my own, I felt good and confident going into the new season. The departure of Mr Struth had signalled a new era for the club and, while it was sad to see him relinquish the control he had exercised for such a long time, I was looking forward to life at Rangers under the new manager. Although the early signs were that it would be business as usual for most of us, I noticed that Symon was more detached from the players than Mr Struth. Latterly we had rarely seen Mr Struth apart from his brief words of encouragement in the dressing room before games, but I always felt that he cared for us individually and collectively. I never sensed that kind of bond with Mr Symon, but in the early stages of his management, I set these misgivings aside. My focus for the new season would be as always – to play well and to bring success to Rangers. The 1954/55 season had not started quite the way Symon had hoped with the loss of Woodburn, but we remained confident. Personally, I felt it could be my year.

11

The Penalty King And An Old Firm Hat-Trick

THE 1954/55 season had got off in fine style for me and by November, I had scored three penalties in three successive matches, which had one newspaper hail me as 'Rangers' Penalty King'. By December, another newspaper had referred to me as 'Scotland's Penalty King' after I had scored my seventh from the spot.

It had all begun, of course, on the North American tour just a few months earlier, or perhaps I should say it began back in South Africa! I was just a ten-year-old schoolboy when I recall that I started having a go at penalties. Then, I was not much bigger than the corner flag, but I found that I could fool goalkeepers as they tried a wrong mind-reading act. To me, that was always the secret of a good penalty – try to dupe the goalkeeper.

As I grew up in Pretoria, moving up the age groups in the different teams I played for, I would always take the penalties as my reputation for being pretty capable from the spot increased. Even while I was the baby of the Berea Park senior team I was given the responsibility of taking the penalties and I never failed. When I arrived at Ibrox, I eventually worked myself into the position of taking all of the penalties for the reserves, where my success from 12 yards continued. It was only when I played for the Rangers first team in the early part of my career, that I was not trusted with that responsibility until the North American tour. From that point on, whenever we were awarded a penalty, the ball was thrown to me without hesitation. My team-mates expected me to score and I duly obliged, except on three rare occasions, which I will explain later.

For all that I have seen lots of players miss penalties over the years and they will continue to do so, I never really saw much difficulty in it. For that reason, when I stood up to the ball I fully expected to score. My reputation was to eventually reach such heights that even the other players saw it as a formality when Rangers were awarded a penalty. There is quite a famous picture of one kick I took in a match against Clyde at Ibrox (the frontispiece of this book). Most eyes will be drawn to me in the centre of the picture, poised after taking the kick, or they may glance to the goalkeeper's despairing dive. However, if you look closely, you will see that the rest of the players are standing in the background with their hands on their hips. Usually, players would be lined up on the edge of the box crouched and ready to run in to capitalise on any rebound from the keeper or the woodwork. Instead, these players were resigned to the likelihood that I would score and, as the picture illustrates, I did. They expected me to score and so did I! Through my Rangers career, including representative matches, I took 63 penalties and scored with 60 of them, missing just three, although I always maintain that I never missed them – the goalkeeper saved them! Surely the keepers must get some credit now and again!

I can recall the circumstances of my first 'miss' quite clearly. I had scored 19 successive penalties when I took to the field in a league match at Airdrie's Broomfield Park on 28 January 1956. Midway through the first half we got a throw-in near to the touchline and I went across to receive the ball from our half-back Willie Rae. He would normally lob the ball to me and I would turn and hit it first time into the penalty box. This was a little routine we always did to get the ball into the centre-forward. As Willie threw the ball to me, I swung around to kick it over my shoulder, but as my foot came up to strike the ball, Airdrie full-back Miller lifted his leg to block it. I kicked the underside of his boot and collapsed on the ground with the searing pain.

With no substitutes allowed in football at that time, we played out the first half and I hobbled into the dressing room. There, our trainer Jimmy Smith attended to me and started to take off my boot. I said, 'If you take it off, Jimmy, I'll never get it back on!' I was sure that it would start swelling when the boot came off so he bandaged up my foot with the boot still on. I went out for the second half still hobbling and then with 15 minutes to go, we were awarded a penalty. Even although I was injured, there was no question that I was the penalty taker and I walked forward, picked the ball up and placed it on the spot. I had never missed one before so I felt obliged to take it and I did have this feeling of invincibility when I took them. In truth, I was not mentally charged up to take it, with the pain in my foot still incessant. I hit the ball quite well to my usual corner on goalkeeper Davie Walker's right, but he anticipated it, dived correctly and made a good save. It had no bearing on the outcome of the match as we won 4-0, but I was disappointed that I had missed.

It was 11 months before I would miss another and this time it came in a match against Kilmarnock at Rugby Park on 22 December 1956. They had Scotland international Jimmy Brown in goal. We were already behind in the match when we were awarded a disputed penalty in the 27th minute to a howl of boos from the Killie fans. I was unfazed as I placed the ball on the spot and then turned to make my run-up. I decided I was going to put it in my usual place, in the goalkeeper's right-hand corner, but as I started to move forward, the referee stopped me. He had noticed some Killie player encroaching on the box, but it disturbed my concentration.

He should have left me to get on with it and called a retake if I missed. However, I started my run-up again and made the fatal mistake of changing my mind which corner I was going to hit it into. I placed the ball to the left and Brown dived correctly to make the save. It was very disappointing, especially since we lost that match 3-2. By then I had a reputation for being pretty lethal from the penalty spot, so it caused a bit of a stir in the press when I missed.

Around that time, I had started on the Scottish Football Association coaching school to get my coaching badges. A few weeks after the Killie match I attended a session at the SFA's training facility at Largs. Jimmy Brown was also there and when he saw me, he started boasting to everyone about how he had saved my penalty in our last game. I suppose it highlights what a big thing it was for a keeper to save one of my penalties, but I was irritated. A little in anger, I said to him that although he had saved that last one, I could take another ten penalties against him and he would not save any of them. As a wager, I offered him a bet of £1, which he would win if he saved just one of my ten penalty kicks – or lose if I scored with every one of them. That was quite a lot of money in these days and obviously the odds were heavily stacked against me – or it seemed that way.

He very readily accepted the bet and we took to the pitch, with a few of the other players watching in amusement. I put the ball on the spot, ran up and then hit it firm and true into my usual corner on his right – the opposite side from the one he saved in the match. As he set up ready for the second one, I once again hit the ball into the right-hand corner. The third went the same place, as did the fourth and then the fifth. By this time there was a lot of psychology in it as he had clearly decided that if I was taking ten, at least one would go to his left. And so, the sixth, seventh, eighth and ninth went to the right and each one landed behind him and in the net. The more I had taken and hit to his right, the more convinced he was that the next one would go to his left.

I had placed the first nine to his right-hand side and each time he had dived to the left. We were now faced with the final penalty. If he saved, he won the bet, if I scored, I had redeemed myself – and earned £1.

I ran up to the ball and hit it firmly into the same corner as the previous nine and Jimmy dived into the opposite corner. He was stunned and I proudly walked back to the dressing room. He never gave me that pound and, although we met lots of times thereafter, as he lived quite near me, there was little mention of our penalty challenge. He was one of the game's great characters and when he died, I thought that it was a terrible way to duck out of his debt. However, I will eventually see him up there and maybe then he will pay me back!

The third and last time I missed a penalty was against Falkirk, who had the great Bert Slater in goal. It came in a league match at Ibrox on 16 March 1957, just a few weeks after Jimmy Brown had saved at Kilmarnock. The conditions were very heavy and the park boggy. Although Slater was a wonderful goalkeeper, he was quite small and I tried to lift the ball to place it higher into the corner. It just made it easier for him and he dived across to make the save.

The headlines of the *Evening Times* read, 'HUBBARD MISSES – Slater raises the roof as he foils the penalty king!' We ended up drawing that match 1-1 and when I came into the dressing room, I said to Scot Symon, 'That's me finished with penalties.' He patted me on the back and said, 'No you're not – you will take the next one.'

I had nothing to celebrate with these three penalties, although on each occasion I forced the keeper into making the save by hitting the target. However, on 60 other occasions, I left the goalkeepers invariably on the other side of the goal with the ball nestling in the opposite corner of the net. I have often been asked about the secret of taking good penalties and I have always said that it is about fooling the goalkeeper even before you hit the ball. For me, the run-up is very important. I admire the modern players and how they approach a penalty, but there are many times that I know exactly where they are planning to put the ball, just from where they are standing prior to the kick. When I took penalties, I never gave the goalkeeper any clues to where I would hit the ball, even though most of the time I hit it low and 90 per cent of the time, to their right. I never looked at the goalkeeper or tried to give him the eye. I would step backwards about four or five steps, taking up a position almost straight behind the ball, but slightly off to my left, allowing me to strike the ball with my right foot. By approaching the ball from a slight angle, you have enough flexibility to hit it left or right. As I walked back, I kept looking at the ball and I continued to look at it as I prepared for my run-up. I never looked at any one side of the goal, or the goalkeeper, but just gazed straight at the ball.

After a few seconds, I started my run to strike the ball with the instep of my right foot. You can get more power on the ball with the instep and the ball is less likely to rise than it would be with a side-foot shot. A side-foot also 'telegrams' the shot, giving the goalkeeper a pretty good idea on where you were likely to put it. Of course, if the goalkeeper dives the right way, then he has a much better chance of saving the ball, regardless of how you hit it, which is why I always tried to disguise my intentions in my run-up. I generally hit the ball firmly enough to hold its trajectory and into the corner of the goal, a couple of feet above the ground. If he guesses correctly and goes the right way, a save is easier if the ball is played too high or conversely on the ground. With a penalty hit high, it is easier for him to reach from a standing position. A low penalty along the ground can be easily saved as the goalkeeper's dive takes him near to the ground with his hands low as he reaches towards the post. A penalty ball hit firmly, two feet off the ground and close to the post is the most difficult for the goalkeeper. That is how I always tried to play it, but it always starts with fooling him to go the other way.

While the whole idea of taking a penalty can be nervy, especially in big matches, I never really suffered nerves when I took them. I think much of that is down to temperament, but confidence is such a big thing in these situations. You must strike the ball well and never deviate from your first choice of where you planned to put it. In most instances when penalties are saved, it is because the whole situation had become too much for the player, particularly if they change their mind in the run-up, just as I had done at Kilmarnock.

Nowadays, I enjoy watching penalties taken and, as I say, I can generally predict where a player is going to put the ball. There are other factors that come into penalties nowadays that we did not have in our day. Goalkeepers certainly have an advantage in the big games through the knowledge they can gain with television coverage. Most of the top goalkeepers have files on how their opponents usually approach penalties. However, it works two ways and some of the best players use the television to watch how goalkeepers move at penalties. I admire those players who watch the goalkeeper as they approach the kick and wait until he reacts, before putting the ball into the opposite corner or straight down the middle of the goal. Penalty specialists such as Chelsea's Eden Hazard or Juve's Andrea Pirlo are among the best at looking for the slightest movement of the goalkeeper, before striking the ball past him.

We did not have the benefit of video cameras when I played, but we did have to contend with a difficulty that the modern player does not have now – the old-style T-ball. That was vastly different from the modern lighter ball used nowadays – especially on a rainy day when it would become sodden and very heavy. On two of the three misses I had, the ball was sodden, and although I would not use that as an excuse, it was a factor. The condition of the playing field can also influence the outcome, and I recall that David Beckham missed an important penalty in a European Championship qualification match against Turkey in 2003, when he lost his footing as he approached the ball. A similar slip also affected Chelsea's John Terry in the Champions League Final in 2008. It did not work out for either Beckham or Terry on those occasions, but they did have the luxury of playing on good playing surfaces most weeks. It did not happen quite like that in Scotland, so if video can favour goalkeepers into making more saves nowadays, life was equally hard for those taking penalties in my day through the changing conditions of the playing field and the ball. All things considered, success in taking penalties needs two key ingredients which apply as much today as they did back then – skill and temperament. I reckon I had both, which gave me a record from the spot that I am very proud of.

With my growing success from the penalty spot and good performances in most games, things were working out well for me in Scot Symon's first season. We had made a good start to the campaign, but then as we moved through the autumn and into the winter months, the team began to misfire. Besides losing Woodburn, the season had also seen Jimmy Duncanson hang up his boots. A very nice man, he was a very good player with Rangers and a big loss, especially in Old Firm matches. He had a great record against our Old Firm rivals, against whom he scored 22 goals in his Rangers career. If one of the stalwarts retired, there were some new recruits added too through the season. In particular, we saw the baptism of Alex Scott, who was a young winger from Falkirk, aged just 16. He also brought in another outside-left, Bobby Cunning, who was signed from Hamilton Academical. Cunning got a chance in a few games when I was out of the side, but never really broke through and eventually left to work in the family business. Symon continued to look to add to his squad.

It seemed that the loss of such experienced players and Woodburn in particular, had knocked the whole team. We struggled to maintain consistency and we stumbled through the early part of the campaign, slipping behind Aberdeen in the league. We lost out in the League Cup and had even lost the first Old Firm game of the season. We would follow a good run of wins with a disappointing defeat and that seemed to be the pattern. Just about every match proved difficult, but we did not expect the obstacles that beset our trip to Tynecastle to face Hearts in December that year.

We were midway through the season and despite our inconsistency, we lay just two points behind Aberdeen, with Celtic a point behind. We knew that Hearts would provide a stern test, since we had not beaten them in the league in the previous season. Their form had also been indifferent, but they were still just two points behind us and well in contention. They were desperate for the points, but we knew that we could not slip up either.

The weather that day was cold and blustery – not ideal for football, but even worse for travelling. On the way to the match, our team bus got caught up in a traffic jam on the old Edinburgh Road. We waited patiently, but there was no movement in the traffic and we became concerned about getting to Tynecastle in time. As the bus sat locked up in the traffic, a policeman approached. He asked who was in the coach and when he discovered that it was the Rangers team he panicked a little. He knew that the traffic was unlikely to move for hours, as the jam was caused by a fatal car crash and this would result in further delay. We feared that the team bus would not get to Tynecastle for the kick-off at 3pm and the look on his face showed that he shared the same concerns. He turned away, having told us that we should leave it with him. Shortly afterwards, he came back with a more senior police officer, who informed us that our bus would be escorted through the traffic and on to Edinburgh in time for the game.

There was a sense of relief, but despite this, it was clear that we were going to be tight for time. With time running short, it was decided that the players should get changed in the bus as it made its way towards the ground. We pulled the kit box inside the bus and got changed as the driver made his way as quickly as possible to Tynecastle. We arrived at the ground with just 15 minutes until kick-off. There was just time for us to get off the bus, take a quick visit to the toilet, and then make our way down the tunnel to the field.

Nobody in the crowd had an inkling of the traumas we faced in trying to get to the game on time. There is no doubt we were unsettled but we still managed to race into a two-goal lead, when Derek Grierson grabbed a double inside the first ten minutes. It was not a convincing performance from us up to that point, although we did manage to retain that lead until half-time. In the second half Hearts seized the initiative and clawed their way back into the game. Then, with just 21 minutes to go, Willie Bauld put the Gorgie side into the lead. Their advantage was short-lived and with just eight minutes remaining, Billy Simpson popped up to grab an equaliser. He followed that with the winner with just a minute to go. It was a fine goal and the Rangers fans were so deliriously happy that they sang long after the final whistle. I had a decent game, but Billy was the hero that day.

On the day, Hearts were unlucky to lose and the newspapers talked of 'robbery', 'points stealing', and even talked of Ali Baba and his henchmen! Perhaps the match reports would have been a bit more sympathetic if they had known about the traumas of our journey to the game.

The result kept us in touch in the championship, but a few weeks later we faced another match that was critical to our ambitions – the New Year fixture against Celtic. It was our turn to be hosts for the Ne'erday match, the game switching between Ibrox and Parkhead annually and there was an all-ticket crowd of 65,000. I felt good going into the game and the game seemed to be finely poised. Little did I realise that this particular match would endear me to Rangers fans for life. It was to be the pivotal moment in my career.

The early exchanges were typically tight as was normal in the fixture, but in the ninth minute, Jock Stein made a hash of a clearance and sliced the ball directly to Rangers' Derek Grierson. He quickly passed it to Billy Simpson, who promptly turned the ball into the net for the first goal. From then, Stein was panicky and both Billy and I had a field day every time we attacked the Celtic defence. It was not all one way traffic, though, because Celtic had their moments too in the first half, and got an equaliser through Fernie. We went in at half-time at 1-1 but in the second half we really started to dominate the game. However, it took until the 72nd minute for us to get the breakthrough.

I think it is best described by *Sunday Post* columnist Jack Harkness who wrote, 'Can a goal keep you warm for a whole year? Because in 12 months' time I'll probably be recording my opinion of the goal of the year and right now I'm sure it'll be the first goal scored by Johnny Hubbard in the battle at Ibrox. Celtic had started off well – but Rangers had scored. Rangers had then come back into the game – but Celtic equalised. And that was the setting when wee Hubbard, starting in the centre circle, took a pass from Billy Simpson. There was a lot of ground and a lot of Celts between Johnny and the goal as he started off on his most amazing run. He was challenged first by Haughney, he soon took the "Mikey" out of him. Over came Jock Stein. He too was left standing by this slippery eel of a Springbok. Onwards and onwards sped Hubbard still with the ball completely under control. Then to crown everything, with the grace of a ballet dancer, he swerved past the diving Bell and walked the ball into the net. Yes, I think that one will stand to the end of the year.'

'Jaymac' in the *Evening Times* also wrote, 'The coolness and calculation that stamped Hubbard's first goal was astonishing in a game where rivalry is so keen, and every move vital and tense. Haughney, Stein and Bell, no doubt, will be the first to admit that they were completely diddled, but not ridiculed.'

The *Glasgow Herald* correspondent wrote, '[Hubbard] jinked round and past Haughney, Stein and Bell, before he walked the ball into the net.'

It was a memorable goal and I look back on it with very fond memories, but I was not finished there. Eight minutes later I got the ball again and beat three players before I passed to Billy Simpson out on the left wing. Billy's cross was strong, but accurate and as I ran in on goal, I chested the ball over the line from five yards out. By now the Celtic fans were leaving in hordes and in the last minute we got a penalty when Derek Grierson was fouled. I stepped up and easily put it away, again to the keeper's right, for my hat-trick. We won 4-1 and our fans were delirious with joy. I was not unhappy myself and yes, for the next few weeks part of Glasgow belonged to me. I was the first foreign player to score a hat-trick against Celtic. In fact, there have not been many players in the post-war era who have scored a hat-trick against our great rivals.

Eventual Manchester United boss Sir Alex Ferguson, who had celebrated his 13th birthday the day before, was at the match and later described my first goal as easily the best he had ever seen. That was very humbling and I have lived off the story of the goal for many years. The fans love to hear me recount it, as I relive the moment, waltzing past Celtic defenders and leaving them floundering in the mud. It was certainly one of these 'once-in-a-lifetime' games and that it happened against our biggest rivals made it all the more special for me – and the fans. It is true that we only got two points for the win that day and, as it turned out we threw them away again in the next match against Motherwell. However, it was a very special day for me and I am sure for everyone else in blue. It gave Scot Symon his first Old Firm victory and, although these goals were not my first in an Old Firm match, there were none more special.

When you play in an Old Firm fixture you never really know what to expect – whether it will be a good game or a bad one for you. But that day and I would have to say most times I played against our Old Firm rivals, I felt good going into the game. It was always easier at Ibrox too and when I scored that famous first goal, I felt on top of the world. It seemed that everything I tried came off for me that day and as the Celtic players began to lose their confidence, I found that mine increased. I had taken George Young on in a one-on-one on this ground in my first trial match and now I was enjoying dribbling around Celtic defenders as if they were not there.

There is no doubt that my special goal and the hat-trick against Celtic were among the very best of highlights in my career. That they were remembered and had such an impression on a young Alex Ferguson also adds to it. Perhaps it increased his hunger to play the game and he went on to become a very fine centre-forward, eventually joining Rangers too. But, as a manager with so many fine players at his disposal, he must have seen some wonderful goals over his career. For him to mark mine against Celtic that day as 'easily the best' he had seen is truly a great honour.

Despite the euphoria of my hat-trick and the heavy defeat of Celtic, the match was to be one of the few highlights of the season. We finished eight points adrift of Aberdeen and even Celtic managed to displace us from second position. The cup competitions provided no more joy for us and we exited from the League Cup at the quarter-final stage and from the Scottish Cup in the sixth round. Rangers are always judged on success and the 1954/55 season did not provide any of the main domestic trophies. Celtic did not win any of the major trophies that season either, but it was hardly a consolation.

We both had one last chance of the silverware before the season was out – in the Glasgow Charity Cup. We were paired in the semi-finals on 7 May and over 44,000 fans went along to Celtic Park to take in the fixture. It was a last opportunity to salvage something from the season. The atmosphere in Old Firm games is usually tense, especially on the terraces and in the stands. However, the players of both teams generally got on pretty well and would mingle even before big matches such as this. On this occasion, I had a game of snooker

– against Celtic's Jock Stein. He was not a bad player, but I was leading when we were called to go down to the dressing room to get ready. It was a bad omen for Stein – I was beating him on the snooker table and a goal just two minutes from the end from Billy Simpson earned us a place in the final. We went on to defeat a spirited Queen's Park side 3-1. I got the first goal and was voted man of the match and Eric Caldow showed again what a fine full-back he would be.

We were presented with the cup by the Lord Provost a few days afterwards and he ventured that we were lucky to win the trophy, since Celtic were the better side in the semi-final. It did not really matter, because the cup would come to Ibrox, although there was a definite sense of disappointment in how the season had ended. Mr Struth had gone and his best players were beginning to leave the scene too. I could sense that things were going to be different at Ibrox and having established myself in the team, I just had to ensure that I remained part of it as Symon continued to look to introduce new players.

The Charity Cup was not the biggest prize on offer that season, but at least it gave us a little moment of glory. Despite the disappointments of the major honours there were some positives for the team that season. We went in to the season with a defence that had to be restructured after Willie Woodburn's career effectively ended with his *sine die* ban in the first week. With Young moving into central defence, it remained solid. Our real downfall was our away record, losing eight games while Aberdeen lost four and Celtic just two. We lost the league match at Parkhead in dramatic fashion, but gave away a lot of points to teams that we should really have beaten. My hat-trick and the victory against Celtic was a highlight, but we lost the value of that win with three away defeats between Christmas and the end of January. That effectively killed off any chance of the title.

The disappointment of the season apart, off the field it was a good time for me as my mom had arrived in March and remained with us for several months. I could not have been happier with my young family and my mother, all living at our new home in 46 Cardowan Drive, Stepps. She would remain with us until September but returned before the winter set in. She found it very cold here and longed to return to the warmth of Pretoria. I did not realise as she left us to head home that this would be the last time I would see her in Glasgow, before she set off on the long journey home – the train to Southampton and then the boat to Cape Town, where she would board the train again to Pretoria.

Just after the season ended, I travelled back to South Africa to play in an exhibition match with some of my compatriots including Ken Hewkins, Alf Ackerman, and John Hewie. The game was to be held as a testimonial for Stanley Matthews, the great Stoke City and England winger. The game was arranged for the Rand Stadium in Johannesburg on 31 May 1955 and there was a big crowd of around 35,000 in the stadium. All of the visiting professionals, including myself, joined Matthews in a select team to face the local Southern Transvaal XI. As a Northern Transvaal boy, it was a bit of a local derby for me in many respects.

The Johannesburg side got off to a bit of a flyer and surged into a 5-1 lead before half-time. We eased our way back into the game and I scored a couple of goals when we got a penalty. I was in line to take it, which would have given me a hat-trick, but the crowd shouted 'Stanley, Stanley'. I turned to him and said, 'You had better take it, Stan.' He stepped up and, you've guessed it – he missed! We still managed to fight back to get a draw with the game ending with a 5-5 scoreline.

Each of the players received £25 for playing in the match, with Stanley receiving the substantial benefit from the gate money. I was well-known in South Africa by then and someone suggested that I, too, should get a benefit match. However, they suggested that to guarantee a big attendance, it would need Stanley to play in the game too and wondered if I could persuade him to play. I called him up and he said that he was very happy to play, but his terms were not on par with what we accepted for his match. He said he would play, but that he wanted 80 per cent of my benefit money. We were keen for him to play, so we accepted his demands and he duly got around £80, while I got £20 in my own benefit match!

It was good playing alongside the man who was to become Sir Stanley Matthews and it started off something of a love affair with Africa for him. In subsequent years, he was to visit the country many times and helped the black communities, particularly in Soweto during the height of apartheid. It was during this trip that I also went back to see my former head teacher, Mr du Plessis, and looked around my old haunts in Pretoria. However, it was no longer my home and I looked forward to returning to Glasgow, the family – and Rangers.

12

Back-To-Back Titles

WITH the disappointment of his first season behind him, Scot Symon went into the close season of 1955 intent on reshaping the side. The last successful team that Struth had built was gradually being dismantled as more and more of Symon's men were introduced. The transformation of the squad would mean the end for some stalwarts and one of the most prominent of these was Willie Waddell. He had given the club 18 years of sterling service as a player and, of course in later years, he went on to become a great Rangers manager, guiding the club to its greatest triumph with the winning of the European Cup Winners' Cup in 1972.

When I had arrived, Waddell was one of the star players. However, I always felt he was a better international player than he was a club player. His Rangers career was often punctuated with injury but that did not stop him from winning four championships and two Scottish Cups. That record would have been so much better but for intervention of the unofficial competitions through the war years. However, although we played in many a great game together, I never really got to know him. In football you tend to develop close relationships with some players and less so with others. In Waddell's case, it would be true to say that we were not close friends and I always found him to be a little aloof. He was a man who very much kept himself to himself and never mixed a great deal with the players he was not close to. He always seemed to be in a hurry to get away at the end of matches and following training. Most times he was among the first to leave the ground and he would often have left by the time some of us had gotten out of the bath. It was just his way of going about things, but I did not dislike him and I am sure that he would have thought similarly of me. We simply did not speak very often, as he had his own group of close associates.

Ironically, there was one time when I did have a long chat with him and it came long after we had both finished our playing careers. We had both been invited along with many others to a reunion of Rangers players from different eras. The event was held in the Edmiston Club, which was once the Rangers Social Club, adjacent to Ibrox. It had been carefully planned by Alex Willoughby, who played for the Light Blues in the 1960s. During the evening I was asked to go up on to the stage to say a few words to the assembled crowd. I spoke about how proud I was to have played for such a great club and I talked of the many great players I had played with over the years, singling out some of those around me for special mention. When I got to Willie Waddell, I remarked that we had spoken more that evening than we had done through the whole period that we were in the same team – and it was true.

After the departure of Waddell, some new players arrived and the first opportunity that they had to show what they could do came in the trial match. As a regular first team player, I played for the Blues against the reserve team, who were in red. We won the game comfortably, but the big talking point after the match was the physical nature of the game. The youngsters and trialists were doing their utmost to impress Symon and there was a shuddering silence from some of the crowd as the heavy tackles weighed in. I came through it fine and there were good performances from the young reserve goalkeeper Billy Ritchie and Alex Scott, who, although just 18, was already established at Ibrox.

While the fans could savour the good performances from some of the younger players, they had been hoping to catch a glimpse of Scot Symon's new and expensive acquisition – inside-forward Sammy Baird. Baird had been signed in the close season from Preston North End, but he was dogged by injury at the start and did not appear in the trials. Symon knew Baird well and when he was manager of Preston, had signed him from Clyde for a fee of around £12,000. Ironically, Symon was lured to the Rangers job just two weeks after signing Baird for the Lancashire club.

When he was safely ensconced in the manager's office at Ibrox, he went back in for Sammy and reputedly paid similar money for him. In those days, that kind of transfer fee was hefty, so there were great expectations of Baird when he joined the club.

Sammy could play at wing-half or inside-forward and it seemed that the plans were for him to play on the left wing alongside me. If we were going to play together, it would have been good to build up some rapport. However, when he arrived, the two of us did not hit it off in the beginning and that was down to a little history that existed between us. Before Baird had been transferred to Preston, I had played against him at Clyde. In his last match for the Bully Wee against Rangers, I had given him a real roasting and we eventually won 5-2. He always remembered how I tormented him that day and I am sure it affected our relationship in the early years.

Following the trial match, the season traditionally opened with sectional ties in the League Cup, when the teams would be drawn in mini leagues, each playing for a place in the quarter-final. We were drawn in a section that included Falkirk, Queen of the South and…Celtic. It was a tough draw, but it gave the fans an opportunity to see two Old Firm matches early in the season, with each of the teams in the sections playing home and away. We opened the League Cup campaign against Falkirk at Brockville, when Symon showed that he was going to place a greater reliance on youth in his side. Alex Scott continued on the right wing and Max Murray, who was acquired from Queen's Park, came in at centre-forward. Eric Caldow was, by now, a fixture in the side and he was joined at the back by Johnny Little. I kept my place in the side and managed to get a couple of goals as we sauntered away to a 5-0 win.

It was a good performance from the team overall and we kept it going into the return match with the Bairns at Ibrox, although they had a bit of a shock in store for us.

They scored three times in a 12-minute spell early in the game, before I scored twice towards the end of the first half, including one from the penalty spot. We ended up winning with a last-minute goal from Max Murray, but there was still no sign of Sammy Baird.

Baird finally made his debut against Queen of the South at Dumfries and was put straight into the side as my partner on the left wing, at inside-left. Although we narrowly won by the odd goal in three, Sammy had a very quiet game. In fact, we both played poorly, but we were selected for the big game the following week – the first Old Firm fixture of the season, at Ibrox. Again, Sammy had a poor match and I was not much better as we lost 4-1, in a miserable performance all round. At the end of the match when we were in the dressing room, Symon said to me, 'What do you think you were doing out there today?' I was angry, because he had singled me out and said nothing to Sammy, who had not played well at all. I replied, 'When you get me a decent inside-forward, I will do my stuff.' That did not go down too well with the manager and my relationship with Symon was never very good, especially after that encounter. For me it was another contrast with the style of Mr Struth. He would never have singled the players out like that, especially just after a game had ended and in front of the rest of the team. Anything that Mr Struth would have to say would always be delivered behind closed doors in his office. That aside, I could take criticism, but not when I was being singled out unfairly as seemed to be the case on that occasion.

Despite the defeat, Symon retained both Sammy and I in the side for the return fixture with Celtic at

Parkhead just a few days later. After our performance at Ibrox, we were not expected to reverse the scoreline, but that is exactly what we did and more – with a 4-0 victory. Sammy was one of the stars, and I had a good game too. It was a turning point for Sammy Baird in his Rangers career, but it was also important for Symon. The season had gotten off to a fine start and we were happy to have qualified for the quarter-final of the League Cup, especially at the expense of Celtic. Rangers' success is always judged relative to that of our greatest rivals and our fans like nothing better than a victory over Celtic. To win so comprehensively at Parkhead, after such a dismal performance at Ibrox, was the boost that everyone needed.

Baird had carried the burden of his transfer fee, but he showed against Celtic that he was a decent player and he would eventually go on to become a key member of our side. Regardless, our relationship was not always the best. I recall once he called me a 'wee b******' and I replied that I would rather be a wee one than a big one. It was not a serious fall-out, just typical of the banter that existed between the players at that time. I am not sure of the background to that one and why he felt obliged to call me a wee 'b', but there were many other similar incidents where we would have a go at each other. Once when we were sitting in the bath after a match, I said to Sammy that there was a crowd of 45,000 inside the stadium today. Sammy replied, 'How would you know?' I said, 'Well Sammy, I counted them when you were on the ball.' It was a little dig at him that day, because sometimes he never gave me the service from the inside position that a winger needs. Then there were the times when that service *did* arrive, but was not the best with his passes going astray and out of the field. I remember one day at training when we were jogging around the track, I broke away and started to run up the terracing. The trainer, Davie Kinnear, shouted, 'Hubby, where are you going?' I shouted back, 'I am training for one of Sammy's passes!'

It might seem from these stories that we did not get on, but it was not always like that and eventually we settled down to become quite good friends. I was never one to harbour a grudge and neither was Sammy. We went on to have some fine matches together and despite his unimpressive debut, Sammy went on to become a great player for Rangers and Scotland. He spent his last years in Bangor and not long before he died just a few years ago, I had the opportunity to visit him when I was in Northern Ireland. We had a good long chat, reliving these great days of the past. That was the last time I saw him and we had a nice time together. As I said, Sammy was a great player for Rangers, even if sometimes I had to climb the terracing for his passes!

There were many other players who would arrive at Ibrox through that season as Symon looked to create his own team. A young wing-half called Jimmy Millar arrived from Dunfermline, although he just made fleeting appearances in the first two years. As I mentioned earlier, Max Murray had also arrived and would contest the number nine jersey with Billy Simpson, but there was another contender who was about to arrive on the horizon – Don Kichenbrand. The big centre-forward was, like me, South African and he arrived from Johannesburg probably on a similar basis – through a referral from someone connected with

Rangers. He came from Benoni, near Johannesburg and played with the local team, but impressed enough to warrant a move to Rangers. He was solidly built and more like a heavyweight boxer than a footballer. He bustled about and had a good shot, but he did not have much poise on the ball. That aside, he was a good player for Rangers and in that first season, he scored 25 goals in 28 games, so he certainly knew his way to goal.

Kich was nicknamed 'the Rhino' and it has been generally believed that it was the fans that came up with that name. Actually, it was me who gave him his famous nickname and the circumstances came around one day as I stood at the front doors of Ibrox with Sammy Cox. Along the road came Kich wearing a light brown hat and sporting some fancy clothes. One of the great boxers in the 1950s was a fighter named Dado Marino, from Honolulu. He was famous for his flamboyant gear and as Kich strolled up to Ibrox, he looked quite the extrovert. Sammy Cox remarked, 'Here comes Dado Marino!' I commented, 'Marino? He looks more like Ma-rhino!' With his overall physique, the name stuck and from then he was known to Rangers fans as 'the Rhino'.

I enjoyed Kich's company and it was nice to have another South African at the club. We used to play golf together, but he had a ferocious temper and hated losing. I remember once when we were playing at Old Prestwick, he missed a putt and threw his putter into the sea! If you know the golf course, you will also know that it is a long throw into the sea. We both loved playing golf and once in 1957, near the end of Kich's time at Ibrox, we got a chance to meet another very famous South African sportsman – golfer Bobby Locke. He was in

Scotland for the Open Championship at St Andrews and, as a three-time champion, there was a lot of interest surrounding him.

Kich, Willie Paton and I went down to Prestwick St Nicholas before the Open commenced, to watch Locke practise. He recognised us as footballers and we got chatting about golf and how he saw his prospects for the tournament. He then kindly invited us to join him for a game later that day. Excitedly, we went back home to collect our clubs and then met up with him again at the Old Course in Prestwick. I had the great honour of teaming up with this great golfing icon in a match against Don and Willie. It was a tremendous experience, even though I had to throw the ball out of the deep cavernous bunker at the third hole. Unsurprisingly, Bobby and I were too good for Kich and Paton!

We were very fortunate to have the opportunity to play with one of the finest players in golf at the time. The occasion was all the more memorable since he went on to win the Claret Jug that week for a fourth time. It was to be the final time that Bobby Locke would win the Open Championship, so it was very special playing with such a true legend of the sport – and a very nice man too.

Another South African golfer I met several years later, when he came to Muirfield in 1959, was the great Gary Player. He was also a nice man, although I did not get the opportunity to play with him. Again, he went on to win the Open that year, so I must have been something of a lucky charm for South African golfers in the competition.

More recently, I also met South African golfing star Ernie Els at the Open, but he did not win the year I met him. Perhaps my magic was wearing off. I found him to be a nice chap too.

Don Kichenbrand remained at Ibrox for just a couple of years before he went off to Sunderland for two seasons. His stay in the UK was short-lived and he eventually went back to South Africa, before returning to Scotland where he played with Forfar for a brief spell. He had a great first season, but when he lost his place to Max Murray, it seemed that he would not get back into the team and that probably prompted his move to Roker Park. A few years ago, just after Rangers signed Maurice Johnston, Don came out in the press to announce that he was a 'secret Catholic'.

I am not sure why he felt that he had to go to the press with that, but it was certainly nothing to do with his short career at Rangers. However, I always got on well with him and in that one season, he played his part for the team.

Another player who arrived at Ibrox that 1955/56 season was Bobby Shearer, who was signed from Hamilton in December 1955 for a transfer fee of around £2,000. I had played directly against Bobby three months earlier when we won 2-1 at Douglas Park in the first leg of a League Cup quarter-final tie. I scored the winner that day and a few days later, we trounced them 8-0 in the return leg at Ibrox. Again I found the net, scoring twice. Bobby had already been linked with Rangers and gave a good account of himself in the first match, but we were well on top in the second. He must have wondered if that heavy defeat would end Rangers' interest, but he did eventually get the move to Ibrox that he probably dreamed of.

Shearer was a good addition to our squad and a bit of a joker, so he was good for morale in the dressing room. I remember once on the eve of the Rangers Sports, we trained at Ibrox while the water jump in the steeplechase was in place. Bobby pushed me into the water and I was soaked from head to toe! I did manage to get some retribution when both Billy Simpson and I duly grabbed him and turned *him* upside down in the water. It was all part of the good fun and atmosphere within the squad and Bobby Shearer was an important part of things when I was there. I was not surprised that he went on to become a great Rangers captain.

After the disappointment of his first season, Symon's revitalised Rangers side began to pay dividends and by September my performances had merited a call-up to play for the Scottish League team against the Irish League. It was to be my first 'cap' and I was joined in the Scottish side by George Young, who also captained the side. The game was played at Ibrox in front of a crowd of over 33,000 and I scored the opening goal – from the penalty spot. We went on to win 3-0 and I was rewarded with another cap a few weeks later when we faced the League of Ireland in a match at Dalymount Park, Dublin, and this time we won 4-1. After such convincing victories, the League selectors stuck with us and I was chosen to represent the Scottish League against a Danish Combination side for a match in Copenhagen on 11th October.

We won 4-0 and I scored the third. It was an easy game against the amateurs, with even the local press saying it should have been 10-0. However, we were to come up against sterner opposition two weeks later on

26 October 1955 at Sheffield – the English League. That marked an important historical milestone when I became the first player from outside the UK to appear in the fixture. It was not a memorable game for either the Scots or me, however, and we lost 4-2.

These four caps certainly boosted my confidence, but the Rangers team had failed to impress in the early part of the 1955/56 league campaign and we went out of the League Cup at the semi-final stage to Aberdeen. By December, however, with the help of a few Kichenbrand goals, we began to turn the corner. We hammered Hibs, who at that time were league leaders and then in the New Year fixture at Celtic Park, the Rhino got the only goal of the game to leave us just a point behind our rivals with two games in hand. By the end of February, big Kich had played in 19 consecutive games and failed to score in just five. At the end of March we were five points clear as Celtic slipped away as Hearts became our nearest challengers. The Tynecastle side had earlier put us out of the Scottish Cup but we felt we were in control in the title race and playing well. We duly completed the campaign with an easy win over Aberdeen at Ibrox to give Rangers the championship for the 29th time and for me it was a second title.

That season was quite unique, because I had played four times for the Scottish League, but on 12 March 1956 I earned my only cap for South Africa in a match against Scotland – at Ibrox. The match was organised to raise money for the British Olympic Games Appeal, but it gave us a chance to get a run-out for our homeland against our adopted home. Kich played, as did John Hewie, Ray Davies, and Ted Purdon, and we almost caused a shock. We lost 2-1, despite being two down at the interval and I scored the South African goal with – yes, a penalty! One of the journalists wrote, 'Hubbard made his usual casual slow-motion scoring job with the penalty kick.' I reckon I probably set some kind of record with that goal, as possibly the only player to score for and against his 'country'. It was a strange experience for Kich and I, because we were cheered by the home support against Scotland.

Although I had watched a number of the seasoned campaigners leave as Symon transformed the team, his approach had certainly proved successful. There were many young players coming through the ranks and I could not be complacent. However, I did not see that I had anything to be concerned about as I had a good season and contributed 27 goals – more than in any other campaign.

After an indifferent start to the 1956/57 season, when we went out to Celtic in the sectional League Cup stages and dropped three points in our opening two league fixtures, we quickly picked up where we had left off in the last season. A win at Celtic Park in the first of the Old Firm league fixtures saw us back on track and by the turn of the year we were well clear of our Glasgow rivals and just behind Hearts, who had surged off to a good start. However, there was an added dimension to that season that none of us had experienced before – competitive European football. As the champions of Scotland, we could gain entry to the revamped European Cup, which was an interesting distraction away from the rigours of domestic football and an opportunity to see how the game was developing on the continent.

After receiving a bye through the first round, we were drawn in the second to face the French title holders, OGC Nice. The first game was scheduled for Ibrox on 24 October 1956 and, although Nice had struggled a little in the first few games of their league season, we knew that they would still be a decent side. However, the naivety of the press was such that they were calling for us to score six goals in the first leg, so that the second leg in France became a formality. It made no difference to us, because we just approached the game as we always did – without any tactics.

It was the way of football at that time. The onus was on the players themselves to work out what their opponents offered and what dangers they presented. For my part, I used to watch the full-back and half-back to see where their strengths lay. Were they weak on one foot and were they quick? Could I beat them for pace and what side should I choose if I was taking the ball past them?

I did this for every match whenever I played against someone I did not know and I imagine my team-mates did the same. Mostly in the Scottish league we got to know the players we would face, but Nice would offer another proposition. For that reason, we were looking forward to playing the French, because it was something different and we would also be playing under floodlights with a big crowd anticipated. We also felt that the timing was right as we were going into the match off the back of some form. We were unbeaten in 13 games, which included two victories over Celtic and I was also in a good seam of form, with 11 goals, including seven penalties.

When the French arrived in Glasgow they took the opportunity of training at Ibrox, which gave many a chance to have a look at them. They were a fit looking bunch and boasted a Riviera tan, but this was October in Glasgow so they would have to contend with a wet pitch. The match proved to be a huge draw for the fans and 65,000 assembled inside Ibrox for the game. They watched us line up virtually at full strength, with George Niven in goal, Bobby Shearer and Eric Caldow at full-back and a half-back line of Ian McColl, George Young and Willie Logie. The forward line included Alex Scott, Billy Simpson, Max Murray, Sammy Baird and myself. Willie Logie, a Canadian, who had made his debut just a month earlier, was the newcomer to the side.

I lined up against quite a distinctive French right-back called Gilbert Bonvin, but if I felt I could contend with anything he offered in a football sense, I was quite unprepared for the roughhouse tactics which he and his team-mates employed. Tackles were flying in from every direction and our players gave as good as they got until the English referee, Arthur Ellis, eventually pulled the two teams together early in the second half. By then, the score was 1-1 after Max Murray had scored just before the break to cancel out the opener from the French, who had taken the lead midway through the first half. After that, the game deteriorated into a bit of a wrestling match rather than a football game, but we tried to continue to play, although Billy Simpson ended up rolling on the ground with Bonvin at one stage.

Billy did manage to get the goal that gave us a 2-1 lead on 61 minutes and from there we pushed forward to try to open up a decent margin. The referee blew the whistle to end the game and as the rain poured down, we headed straight up the tunnel while the ball boys collected the flagpoles from the corners. We were in the dressing room and I had my jersey off, while some of the boys were in the bath. Then, the referee came in to tell us that he had made a mistake and stopped the game early. We had to get back out on to the field to play another five minutes or so. By then, we had lost all our momentum after this farcical blunder and we could not add to the score. We were left to lick our wounds and rue that we had lost an opportunity to score many goals. Nice were a decent side but we should really have sewn up the tie that night.

We were scheduled to meet Nice the following Wednesday and even arrived in France ready for the game, but the worst weather that city had endured in years forced a postponement of the match for two weeks. By the time we eventually managed to get back to France a fortnight later – which took a 12-hour plane journey via a stopover in Paris – the weather in the Cote D'Azur remained anything but Mediterranean. Persistent rain turned the pitch into a pond, which did not suit either the French or ourselves. When we took to the field, we were unchanged from the first leg and, although conscious that we had to protect a lead, there was simmering bad feeling. For our part, we resolved to play football and not get involved in any retaliation, although we expected that there would be more of the roughhouse tactics from the French.

When the game kicked off, we were playing into the wetter part of the pitch – or the deep end as it might have been called! I had a shot which seized up in a puddle and then as I made a few runs at the Nice defence I was cut down repeatedly. Then, with just about half an hour gone, I almost scored, but the Nice keeper brought out a wonderful save. A few minutes later, Max Murray cut into the box and was tripped as he was about to shoot. It was a penalty. The decision sparked a barrage of protests from the Nice players and also caused a bit of disturbance in the French crowd. Missiles rained on to the pitch as the referee held up the game, while the police tried to restore authority.

The game must have been delayed by at least seven minutes and most people had eyes on the terracing and all of the disruption. Few people noticed the Nice goalkeeper creep up to the ball which I had placed on the spot a few moments earlier. He swept the chalk from the penalty spot with his hand, when most were distracted by the crowd and he then placed a little mound behind the ball.

When order was restored I prepared to take the kick. I started as if to make my run-up and then as I reached the ball, I stopped. I bent down to move the ball to one side, while the referee looked on. He could see the little mound of earth, which had been placed by the French goalkeeper. I picked it up, then walked over to the keeper before lobbing it towards him underhand. The keeper dodged this little mass of earth that came flying towards him, as the referee watched impassively. He obviously knew what had happened and took no action. I replaced the ball and then strode up before hitting it firmly past the keeper and into the right-hand corner of the net. The incident did not really bother me at all, although the Nice keeper was obviously trying to distract me. I dealt with it in the simplest way possible – by scoring to put us 1-0 ahead.

We had given ourselves a two-goal advantage but we threw it away in the second half and Nice levelled the tie at 3-3. To compound matters, Willie Logie was attacked by two of the French players near the end and as one put a fist on his chin, Willie raised his hands in defence. The Frenchman was ordered off and Logie went with him for retaliation, when he had done no more than protect himself. It was hard justice on the youngster as he had been at the centre of much of the harsh play from the Nice defenders. At that time, European ties were not settled on away goals, so the game went to a replay. We limped off the pitch with more than bruised pride. I had six bruises on my legs and a large lump.

The replay was held in the Parc des Princes two weeks later and Nice won 3-1. It was disappointing and our plans were disrupted by the absence of George Young, who was laid low with a virus. However, his replacement Harold Davis had a fine game, so we only had ourselves to blame. There was a distinct disappointment in losing a tie that we should have closed out in the first leg. Despite the defeat, we had a taste of European football and wanted more. If anything, it served to spur us on to win the championship again and gain entry once more. My consolation was that I would go down as the first Rangers player to score in an away tie in Europe, but it was a meagre reward for the efforts and pain of those three ties. Nice may have disposed of us, but they tumbled out in the next round at the hands of the reigning champions, Real Madrid. We were not disappointed.

From the turn of the year we remained unbeaten in the league and secured the championship once again by beating Queen of the South at Palmerston in the penultimate game for back-to-back titles. I opened the scoring from the penalty spot on 15 minutes and we went on to score twice more. Ironically, it was where I had enjoyed my first title win and now I had three medals after a trio of championship wins. We did not celebrate that day, because we knew that our win could have meant relegation for the Doonhamers, but as it turned out, they managed to get the points they needed for safety in their final match. Although the title was secured with that win in Dumfries, the pivotal match came just a few days earlier at Hampden where we faced Queen's Park. It was probably one of the most dramatic games I had played in.

Early in the match, Queens got a penalty and missed. It did not affect their composure and they were playing the best football in the first half. So much so, that with just around five minutes left to the interval, they were 4-1 ahead! Not many people would have given us much hope of the title at that stage but in that short spell before the break, I scored twice. When the second half resumed, goals from Max Murray, Billy Simpson and Alex Scott gave us what seemed at one stage to be an unlikely 6-4 win. It was to be the last appearance at Hampden for George Young, the final old-timer of the Struth era, who hung up his boots at the end of the season. He had been a wonderful servant for club and country and his career ended in the best way possible with that title win.

With Young gone, there were few around the squad that had been there when I first joined Rangers. Indeed, only Ian McColl remained as a part of the side, in which

I was now one of the most senior members at just 26. It was a good time for Rangers though as we celebrated those back-to-back titles and had that first taste of Europe. The next season could not come quick enough for me and I was sure it would be another good one.

13

The Clouds Gather

WITH George Young retired, Ian McColl was handed the captaincy of this new and exciting Rangers team. I missed the trial match through an ankle injury but the youngsters again made their mark, with Davie Wilson deputising for me. In defence, young John Valentine was given the unenviable task of replacing George Young, but most felt we would dominate Scottish football once again. It certainly seemed that way in the early part of the season as we safely negotiated our way through the League Cup sectional ties and our European Cup first round match against St Etienne. It was something of a false dawn for the next few weeks brought quite different fortunes for us.

In September, we lost our first Old Firm league match at Ibrox in over 20 years, 3-2, but at that stage in the season we were not overly concerned. What did alarm us more was the result when we faced Celtic in the League Cup Final just four weeks later. The result which sent a shudder through every Rangers fan, was a 7-1 defeat. It was a freak result and there were never so many goals in the game. In fact, it was very even up to the last 30 minutes, although we were 3-1 behind at that stage. Celtic had gone in two ahead at the interval, but it was just one of those games when it seemed that every time they mounted an attack, they scored. Young John Valentine was the scapegoat and within a few games lost his place to new signing Willie Telfer from St Mirren.

Billy Simpson scored our only goal on that disaster of an evening and we used to have a bit of banter around that. He claimed to be absolved from any responsibility over the result, since he scored, but I used to say if he had put away the seven chances I created for him in the game we would have won 8-7! It was a little bit of humour surrounding a game that was anything but humorous.

Within a few weeks, we also tumbled out of the European Cup at the hands of Inter Milan and by the turn of the year, I had lost my place to Davie Wilson. That meant a couple of months on the sidelines, before I came back into the side in February with my new inside-left, Ralph Brand. By then we were already well behind the league's pacesetters, Hearts. Our challenge was severely impacted by a backlog of fixtures. European football had been a great experience but between these matches and the campaigns in the League Cup and Scottish Cup we were six games behind Hearts in the programme. The championship was lost and, after losing out to Hibs in the semi-final of the Scottish Cup, our season was virtually ended weeks before the official close on the season.

In the closing months of that 1957/58 season I went to the SFA's training facility at Inverclyde, Largs to take my coaching badges. The coaching sessions were led by the association's chief coach, Dave Russell, who had won the Scottish Cup with East Fife in 1938 as a player. He had coached in Denmark after the war and then went to Bury, building a good reputation which obviously attracted the SFA hierarchy. I enjoyed working under Russell and he told me that if I ever became available at Rangers, he would be interested in signing me. I thought little of it, because I was firmly focused on continuing and progressing my career at Ibrox, even though I was aware that things were changing.

By the time we entered the close season of 1958, I was already aware that my position in the first team was under threat from Davie Wilson, even though the emerging young winger was serving in the Army. However, I was unprepared for the arrival of another contender for the outside-left position – Andy Matthew, who was signed from East Fife in July for a fee of £4,500. Matthew was Symon's third signing from his old club, adding to Sammy Baird and Harold Davis, who arrived in 1956. More players arrived as Symon continued the construction of his team. Bill Paterson came from Newcastle United and he was joined by youngsters Norrie Martin and Davie Provan. Symon also added a young Craig Brown who was to go on to become Scotland manager. I kept my head down and got on with training, although I was very conscious that this was an era of new players and that the older guard were being marginalised. In particular, it seemed to me that I had fallen out of favour and that I had a battle on my hands to retain the number 11 jersey.

As usual, the first airing for the players at the start of the season was the Rangers Sports five-a-side and I was selected in the team alongside Eric Caldow, Bobby Shearer, Alex Scott and Sammy Baird. We beat Clyde 1-0 and I scored the only goal – from the penalty spot! A few days later, I played for the Blues in the trial match, but for the first time in years, we lost out 3-2 to the Reds. I felt I played well enough, but some of the youngsters pushed hard for a permanent place. Come the Saturday for the first of the sectional League Cup ties, against Hearts, I was selected at outside-left with Davie Wilson, who had managed to get a pass from the Army, at inside-left. We won the game comfortably, 3-0, and I scored a good goal in open play. After the game, one pundit reckoned that I was the best forward on the field.

As the season moved on to October, it was clear that despite my performances for the side, both Wilson and Matthew looked to be increasingly favoured by Symon. I knew that my time at Ibrox was almost over and, from then, my Rangers career seem to fade and die in quite unassuming circumstances. We played against Clyde in the Glasgow Cup Final on 22nd October 1958 and a poor team performance saw us lose by an early goal. We dominated the match, but could not get the ball in the net. It was the second disappointing draw at Ibrox in four days as we had lost a late goal to drop a point against Raith Rovers on the Saturday. After the match, both Sammy Baird and I were dropped along with young George Duncan, a fringe player. Others could easily have found themselves left out, but Symon wanted his scapegoats and I was one of them. I was replaced by Andy Matthew, although it might as easily have been Wilson. I had no doubts now that both were preferred ahead of me with Wilson probably the number one. It was obvious to me that if Wilson was not selected, the jersey would be passed to Andy Matthew. From then, both Matthew and Wilson shared the jersey.

The Raith Rovers match may have ended in a disappointing draw, but it did signal the debut of Iain McMillan, who had been signed from Airdrie for around £10,000. I know that Iain was to prove a revelation for Alex Scott on the right wing, as a winger relies on a good inside man. Iain went on to become a great player with the club and eventually formed a great partnership with Willie Henderson. I was sorry that I did not get the chance to play many games in the same team as him. After his debut against Raith Rovers, we were only to play three more times together.

After the Glasgow Cup defeat by Clyde I did not feature in the side again for four weeks, until we played against Grasshopper Club of Zurich in a friendly match on 25 November 1958. Even then, my return to the side was necessitated because of an injury to Matthews. We won 3-0 and I scored with a penalty – again – but it was a quiet night for me. I was restored to the position again on the Saturday against Motherwell at Fir Park, and I had a much better game, scoring Rangers' equaliser in a 2-2 draw. By the time the next game came around, however, I was on the sidelines once again with Davie Wilson back at number 11. I found being number three in line for the jersey hard to deal with, even though I was the club's joint top goalscorer with 13 goals – not a bad total to accumulate before the end of November. In fact, that was 13 goals from just 14 games, while Davie Wilson went on to play 22 games that season scoring just four times, with Andy Matthews scoring seven from 21 matches. I was obviously the most prolific of the three of us and felt I had played well in the early part of that season. My opinion counted for nothing, however.

I continued to train without any sign of being included and watched Symon shape his new side and discard those he felt that he no longer needed. Among them was my great friend Billy Simpson who was transferred to Stirling Albion in March. Billy was my best pal in Ibrox at the time and it seemed that more and more of the old faces were being phased out. Billy had seen his own place threatened by Jimmy Millar and Max Murray and found his appearances becoming limited. I was obviously in a very similar position and I found myself more and more in the wilderness.

I was very sorry to see Billy leave Ibrox. He was one of the real characters and we used to have great banter, even up until recent times when illness took its toll on him. I would often ask him why I got paid £12 per week in the season and £10 in the summer, while he got £14 through the season and then £12 through the summer months. I would say to him, 'Why did you get £2 more than me Billy?' Billy would reply that he was paid more because he was a better player than me. But, I would say, 'You weren't a better player in the summer, Billy!' It was all good banter, of course, and we used to use that little routine often when we spoke at supporters' clubs and other functions.

We had lots of fun together at these supporters' nights and another story we used to tell concerned the two greyhounds that he had. One day he told me that the two dogs would race at the Kilmarnock greyhound track and I should come along. He told me that the first dog that he was running had no chance because he 'had stuffed it'! Basically, he had fed it just before the race to slow it down, which is what a number of owners used to do to get the odds lifted on their dogs for the next race event. Against his advice, I told him I would put a bet on it, because it was showing at 25/1 against. When the race was 'off' the dog started slowly and the leaders were clear, but they collided, allowing Billy's dog to come through and win.

His next dog, which was favourite at even money and had Billy's hopes (and money) riding on it, was slow out of the trap and just failed to cross the line first. I went home with my wallet full after the loser won and I never got invited back again. Despite that, we were always together and would play snooker after training every day. Billy and his wife Margaret would come to our house many times. The last time I saw him was on my 80th birthday, but I made the decision then that I would not see him again. By then, he had deteriorated quite severely and his memory was fading. I wanted to remember Billy as he once was and not the shadow of a man I saw then. It was very upsetting seeing my good friend like that, but I have very happy memories of Billy.

After Billy had left Ibrox, it was clear that I, too, was not favoured by Symon. I worked away training as hard as ever, but I began to realise that there was no place for me at Ibrox anymore.

At 27 years of age I was probably at my peak like most players at that stage in their career. However, Symon had never been my biggest fan and I always felt that he looked for any opportunity to leave me out. I always knew that to stay in the side I had to play well and with even the slightest downturn in form, I would be on the sidelines. The writing was on the wall that my days at Ibrox would be limited. If I could only manage 14 games and could not find a place in the side from October, the chances of returning to the side in the next season looked remote. I decided that the situation could not go on and climbed the Marble Staircase and knocked on Scot Symon's door. As I entered the room where it all began for me, the sense of excitement I had experienced when I met Mr Struth all those years ago, had completely gone. For all the respect I had for the legendary Rangers boss, I could not summon anywhere near that admiration for Scot Symon. As he peered over the desk, I told him that it was obvious that he was not going to play me and I had decided to leave. I told him that I wanted to be put on the transfer list and I would leave at the end of the season. He did not look disappointed and he showed no inclination to try to change my mind. Did he want me to leave? Yes, I believe he was happy to get rid of me. I was one of the last of the Struth men and I genuinely believe that he wanted to surround himself with his own players.

While Symon was glad to place me on the transfer list, the decision was not met with universal approval at board level. As I left the manager's office, the chairman Baillie John Wilson met me in the corridor and told me that he did not want me to leave. It was a nice gesture that I greatly appreciated. Perhaps if Symon had shown the same interest in keeping me, I might have stayed, but there was no point.

The Baillie asked me why I was leaving. I told him that Symon seemed to treat me differently from the other players. He asked if I would stay and I said that I would only remain if Symon had gone and if it got down to a choice between me and the manager, I knew that he would not get rid of Symon.

Although I was lined up to leave in May, the end of my Rangers career still came as a big surprise, as much by the timing and circumstances as anything else. I was laid up in bed with tonsillitis when Scot Symon called. He asked if I was coming in to Ibrox next day and then explained that Bury wanted to sign me. The Bury boss, Dave Russell, had heard of my availability and within a few days of my transfer request, he had approached the club.

Bury were in the English Third Division and I had heard that Manchester City, Cardiff City, Sheffield United and even Hearts wanted to sign me. Whether the fee was the problem or not, it did not matter to me. I presume Rangers notified clubs of my availability and Dave Russell had no hesitation in following up the interest he had first shown at the SFA coaching course.

I would have loved to have stayed with Rangers, but it was not the club I joined under Bill Struth. I was clearly not valued by Symon and there was no future at the club any more. I liked Dave Russell and the move to Bury to work under him was attractive. He was a good man – a different kind of character from Symon – and, while I was sorry to leave Rangers, I was glad to be joining a club and a manager who may appreciate me more.

When I announced my decision to leave Rangers, I had no regrets, although I would leave many friends behind in Glasgow. I had been effectively frozen out of the team and, at just 27, I knew that I had many years ahead of me in the game. I had played with Rangers at the top level, but I could not sit on the touchline knowing that my prospects of playing were limited. It is very difficult for a player when you train hard each day, but feel that there is a barrier to a place in the first team.

To be fair to Symon, he was building a good team and Rangers took the championship that season. I had played a part in that success even if it was not quite as big a role as I either wanted or expected after the start to the season. There were new players in the team and all of the top team were re-signed, with Billy and me the only ones of note to depart at the end of that season.

However, in my mind, I did not really leave Rangers. You can never leave Rangers, because the club remains in your heart, but I left Symon. That is why I often say when asked about my departure, 'I never left Rangers, just Scot Symon.'

I looked forward positively to Bury, even though it was a step down the leagues for me. I was conscious that they had paid £9,000 for me, which was their biggest fee in years, and I wanted to ensure that I rewarded them. I looked forward to the prospect of playing with them. Rangers had changed from the club I first found when I arrived ten years earlier into Mr Struth's cradle. I would miss many things about the club, including Ibrox and the fans who had always been good to me. However, I now had to look south towards my move that would be made in the close season. We put our house in Cardowan

Drive up for sale and it was sold for £1,720 – the same sum we paid for it. I had so many happy memories of Rangers, Glasgow and Scotland, but now it was time to move on. I was excited as we packed our bags and headed to Lancashire, for a new start.

14

Life After Rangers

THE move to Bury proved to be a good one both professionally and personally. We bought a nice home at 40 Rhiwlas Drive in the town, just a few hundred yards from Bury's ground at Gigg Lane. My family settled into our new surroundings very well and we both met some nice friends locally. That was very important to us as we had uprooted everything. At the football club, everything was good too. I felt refreshed with life under Dave Russell's coaching. Importantly, Russell was also a lovely man and I was settled at a club with a manager who valued me.

In contrast to the training at Ibrox, which never changed throughout my ten years at the club, Bury's sessions were tremendously varied. Not only did the training sessions themselves change, but so did the venue. On some days we would train on land at the golf course, then on other occasions we would take to a park somewhere else in the town. Each day we turned up for training, we had no idea where we would be going and this was refreshing, ensuring training was always interesting and enjoyable. However, the most impressive part of our training sessions was the meticulous planning that Dave Russell put us through as he analysed the opposition. He would sit us all down and then go through the opposition's players and style, using the blackboard to illustrate his tactical approach. The last time I had seen a blackboard in use was at primary school!

At Bury, they put huge thought into the forthcoming matches and I enjoyed that meticulous approach. We would discuss who we might face in the game and what their strengths and weaknesses were. I reflected back on the training at Ibrox under Jimmy Smith, Joe Craven and Davie Kinnear. At Rangers, the focus was on fitness and playing short games, with little time spent in discussing the opposition. Dave Russell was a great coach at the SFA and I felt that his skills shone through like a beacon at Bury.

I went straight into the side, secure within my favoured position on the left wing. I was also renowned as 'The Penalty King' and was trusted to take the spot-kicks for Bury too. We did not get as many penalties as we did at Rangers, but it was nice that my reputation went before me. I never missed one at Bury.

The Bury fans were desperate for the team to get promoted after being relegated to the Third Division for the first time in their history in 1957. We had a good start to the season and by the beginning of October with a third of the games behind us, we were in a pack just three points off the lead. By Christmas, we were just a point off the leaders Southampton, with a few chasing teams only a few points behind. A month later we surged to the top although Southampton had a few games in hand. It was shaping up well though and I was enjoying my football. Then came an incident that I was completely unprepared for – match-fixing.

In recent times, two Rangers players were disciplined by the Scottish Football Association for betting on football matches, which was a breach of the governing body's regulations. I gather that the instances did not relate to matches in which Rangers were involved, but it was unwise in any case. The players were embarrassed at least by the revelations, but I saw the seedier side of betting in that first season at Bury.

In February 1960 we had continued to hold our narrow lead at the top of the league and although Southampton had slipped back, Norwich City and Coventry remained hard on our heels. We were due to play an away match against Barnsley at their Oakwell ground which promised to be a tough tie, even though the Tykes were mid-table. They were coming off the back of a 5-0 defeat at the hands of Halifax Town so they had a lot of incentive to get their season back on track against the league leaders. However, we were going into the match having lost 3-0 at home to Swindon Town a week earlier, so we wanted to maintain our place at the top of the table.

In the week leading up to the match, everything was normal in our preparations until one day I was approached by a man I had never seen before as I left training at Gigg Lane. I cannot remember much of the conversation other than he said that he would offer me and the team money if we lost the game against Barnsley by a 4-0 scoreline. He offered me £6,000 which he said would be split between me and the players if I could help to arrange things. I would get £3,000 for helping to get some of my Bury team-mates involved and they would share the remaining £3,000. I was shocked and quite taken aback. I immediately told him that I was not interested, but the whole situation was quite sinister. I hardly slept for thinking about what had just happened and I decided that I should tell the club immediately.

The next day, I went straight to the manager Dave Russell, who then told the directors. I left it with them and never heard any more. I never saw the man again and, by then, with the club alerted to the situation, any chance of any match-fixing had gone. It made us all the more determined to win the match at Barnsley, although we ultimately had to share the points when the game finished 2-2. Prior to that incident, I had never heard of any match-fixing and it was completely against my ethos. I played every game to win and I was appalled that there were people out there who would try to engineer the result of a match for their own financial benefit. I had no further approaches and the guy obviously realised that there was never any chance that I would contemplate getting involved in anything like that. However, it was not the last time I was to hear of match-fixing in England.

A few years later there was a lot of drama around a major scandal that involved a syndicate of players who were engaged in the manipulation of games. The one man who seemed to be at the heart of it all was a former Scots player, Jimmy Gauld, who had ended up at Mansfield Town in England after starting his career at Pittodrie. He also had a short spell at St Johnstone, but his notoriety came when he hung up his boots in 1961. He apparently set up a betting syndicate of players from around the divisions who were enticed to throw matches. It was all done the same way as the approach to me. A player was singled out, then others were drawn into the web by that player. The scam was eventually uncovered and Gauld sold his story to a Sunday tabloid, incriminating lots of other players, including some England internationals. The police took up the story from there and several players were banned with some finding themselves in jail. Among them was Gauld, who got four years in prison in 1965.

It is a story that is quite frightening from a number of perspectives. Whether Gauld was behind that first approach to me, I do not know, but it gave me some insight to what was to happen in the game a few years later. It may have been that some matches around my time were fixed, but if so, they were not obvious. In any case I do not know how I could influence a match to lose 4-0, except with the help of many players. I had been reared with a determination to succeed and I would not have ended up at Rangers without that inherent will to win at everything.

Whoever approached me to try to fix that game clearly did not know me, but I was the last to entertain such thoughts or get involved in a betting scam.

Those behind the scam presumably did not get their money on Barnsley to win that day. For Bury, by coincidence, the fine start to the season we had enjoyed began to disintegrate from then onwards and we did not pick up a victory in the last five games of the season. It was a disappointing end to a season that offered a lot of promise. We had failed to maintain the momentum, but at least our defeat was an honest one.

The disappointing ending apart, that first season at Bury was a good one for me as I settled into the side. However, 1960/61 was to become not only a decent season for me, but a record-breaking one for the club. Bury secured the most points and the most goals ever accumulated in a season on their way to winning the Third Division in style. We had lost out in the run-in the previous year but the experience stood us in good stead. It had helped to build a good harmony among the players and we were a pretty tight-knit group. I was playing well and was popular with the fans. The forward line in particular had a good rapport. We had all been introduced to the side about the same time and we were a prolific bunch too. Of the 108 goals that the team scored that season, the forward line got a remarkable 99. Of that total I scored 17.

There were a couple of Scots in the team too – the full-backs Eddie Robertson and Bob Conroy, who had both joined Bury from junior football. They were both small but very formidable. My inside man was Allan Jackson, who remains a good friend to this day. We often chat on the phone, as he still lives in England. Another of my good friends in the team was Brian Turner, a great player who was a half-back with the side. He was a nice chap who mixed well with everyone – and he was a good player too.

For all that I enjoyed life at Bury and, in that first couple of years found the great management and coaching from Dave Russell quite refreshing, my heart still lay with Rangers. Every weekend I would look out for the scores from Scotland and I even managed to catch a game when Rangers came down to the Midlands in 1961 to face Wolverhampton Wanderers in the European Cup Winners' Cup semi-final. That evening as I sat in the stand I met a keen Rangers fan who was in the early stages of his own football career with St Johnstone. His name was Alex Ferguson and he talked glowingly of my memorable goal against Celtic!

I remember the following season when we were promoted into the Second Division, we looked forward to doing well, but things were very much harder. There were a lot of good teams in the league that year and none better than Liverpool. They were by far the best side in the division and when we went to meet them at Anfield, we knew that we were in for a tough game. However, it was harder than we expected! Brian Turner got injured in the warm-up and had to pull out after the teams had been declared. With no substitutes allowed at that time, we had to play the leaders with just ten men from the start. Liverpool went on to win 5-0 and they maintained their dominance to go on and achieve promotion to the First Division that season. There were four Scots in the Liverpool team that day, including Tommy Leishman, Ian St John, Ron Yeats and, in goal, Bert Slater. Bert was one of the few goalkeepers to have saved one of my penalties, when he was between the sticks at Falkirk.

Another famous Scot at Liverpool at the time was their manager – Bill Shankly. I remember once that I had the opportunity to spend a good couple of hours with him on a train. Bury had played in London that day and Liverpool were also in the south and heading back north. By coincidence, the two teams were on the same train and I shared a carriage with Shankly. He talked about football constantly and I was completely taken with the intensity of his interest in the game. He talked incessantly and I could hardly get a word in, so much so that all I could do on that long journey back to Lancashire was to nod, say yes, or add no!

By December, the team was languishing in the bottom half of the league and manager Dave Russell decided he had had enough and quit to take over at Tranmere Rovers. It was disappointing, but the club had already identified a replacement – my team-mate, Bob Stokoe. He had joined from Newcastle earlier in the year and the board saw enough in him to make him player-manager. It was the start of a good career in management for him and he went on to make his own little piece of history when he led Sunderland to the FA Cup Final and victory over Leeds United in 1973. Bob was a decent manager for us at Bury and he succeeded in his main task, which was to keep us in the Second Division. We ended up mid-table, which was as much as we could hope for after the dismal start we had to our campaign.

After the baptism of his first year in management, Stokoe started to rebuild the side. I was 31 and while I still had a few years in me, I think the manager wanted to instigate some changes. He probably wanted to build a team for the future. To his credit, Stokoe approached me at the end of the season to find out what my future plans were. He said that he was aware that my children were growing up and that he imagined that I may want to take them home to Scotland for their education. I thought it was a sensible idea and both Ella and I thought that it was a good move. Bob Stokoe emphasised that he did not want me to leave, but in view of my service to the club, they would release me on a free transfer if I wished to go.

The move was timely, because we did have an urge to return to Scotland. We had made many moves in a short time and I felt we were getting to the stage where we needed to settle down once and for all. Although Stokoe had said he would release me on a free, eventually I discovered that there *had* been a transfer fee involved that earned me about £1,700. The club that came in for me was Ayr United, who were managed by Gerry Mays, who had been a star with Kilmarnock through the 1950s.

I travelled north to meet Mays and found him to be a very nice man. We had a long chat, when he told me of his plans for Ayr United and how I could have a great future at Somerset Park. I knew that Ayr United were at a much lower level than the great Rangers side I had left, but they offered the opportunity to return to Scotland and Ayrshire looked a nice place to live. I had a chat with Ella and we agreed that it would be a good move for us to a nice part of the country. The transfer also gave us the opportunity to buy a house in Prestwick, with a shop below, which Ella planned to run as a small grocers. It all seemed ideal – the family would settle in Ayrshire where the kids would continue their schooling. I had a new football club with a manager who seemed to have some good ideas and Ella had a little business that she could attend to while I was at training, continuing my professional career back in Scotland where it had all begun.

It did not take long for me to find out that Ayr were a poor side, and, if football was tolerable there when Mays was the manager, it became completely intolerable when he left within a year to be replaced by 67-year-old Neil McBain. Although McBain arrived with management experience from a number of clubs, including Ayr in the 1930s and again in the 50s, he was as poor as Symon in my eyes. We did not get off to the best of starts when we prepared for his first match as boss, against Stenhousemuir. His pre-match briefing to me was along the lines of, 'All I want you to do is run down the wing and cross the ball into the box.' There would have been no difficulty in that in normal conditions, but there was a fierce gale blowing across Ochilview Park that day. I told him that the crosses could end up anywhere, but he snapped, 'Don't argue with me!' He was clearly trying to impose himself and was not prepared to listen to me, regardless of my credentials.

So I followed instructions and early in the game I ran down towards the byline and floated a cross towards the centre of the box. On any other day the delivery would have landed just outside the six-yard box, but the wind caught the ball and it drifted over the bar and into the terracing. A few minutes later, I got the ball again and darted towards the line, but this time I hit the cross towards a point outside the box. The wind caught it again and, once more it drifted out of the field. When I got the ball again and reached the line I decided that the only way I could keep it in the park was if I hit it towards the centre circle! This time it went straight, with no effect from the wind and looked ridiculous. You have to adapt your game to the conditions and it was clear to me that, although McBain had been a wing-half in his playing days, he had no idea about wing play.

It was not my best start with McBain and I quickly found myself out of favour. After one freezing night training, I went to see him to ask for a tracksuit top, but also to enquire why I was not selected for the team. He told me that I was not good enough. Our relationship descended further when I asked if the club would pay my National Insurance stamp. He said that he expected it would be paid through my shop earnings, but that was in Ella's name. They had no obligation but to pay my stamp but they decided that if this was going to happen I would need to be full-time. My normal two-nights-a-week training was supplemented with four mornings through the week. I should have got fitter, but I was training alone and I could not get the fitness levels up without someone driving me on. When I eventually returned to the team, I had been out of normal training for so long that I was shattered after ten minutes.

We were a poor side under McBain and he eventually left with more than a hint of controversy that also saw some directors resign. I cannot recall the details of the trouble, but it concerned some discipline that he had delivered to one of our players who failed to turn up at the ground for treatment. I am not sure of the rights and wrongs of that, but he was a confrontational character and it did not surprise me when he left as he did.

Thankfully, McBain was not at Ayr for long and when he left he was replaced by Bobby Flavell in late October 1963. Like McBain, Flavell had managed at Ayr in the past, although only briefly before Gerry Mays took over. He had a good record as a player with many Scots clubs, but most notably Hearts, Dundee and Kilmarnock. But, as a manager, he had made his mark by leading St Mirren to the 1952 Scottish Cup Final. For me it was just good to see a change of boss and I found Bobby Flavell to be a good man. I think he realised the injustice of McBain's team selection and I was immediately reinstated to the side. It was a new start in many ways, but I was by now 32 and nearing the end of my career. There was still time to make my mark in some way, although competition at the highest level seemed to be more of a dream than a reality nowadays.

An opportunity to make some kind of impact on the teams from the First Division came in February 1964 when we were drawn to meet Aberdeen in the Scottish Cup at Pittodrie. We were still not a great side at that time and languished at the bottom of the table. We travelled up by train and when we reached the Granite City, the manager told us we had to walk to the ground. It was a contrast from my time at Ibrox, when taxis would be organised at the station. As we walked to the ground, four of us popped into a bookmakers we passed on the way. One of the guys had a tip for a race and we piled on to the favourite. We listened to the race and, to our delight, the horse surged home first. Since the bookies would be closed by the time the match ended, we waited for our winnings. However, these could not be paid until the jockey had weighed in, so we stood anxiously waiting, all the time aware that the clock was ticking.

Eventually the result was confirmed and we then ran down the road to Pittodrie with the money stuffed in our wallets. By the time we got into the ground it was 2.40pm – 20 minutes before kick-off! An angry Bobby Flavell rounded on us when we arrived in the dressing room, asking where the **** we had been. We told him the truth but there was no time to elaborate as we quickly got stripped ready to play. When we ran on to the field, we were still shaking from the run down the road. If it was far from ideal preparation, the outcome was a shocker – for Aberdeen! We won the game 2-1 to the delight of the small band of Ayr fans and a stunned boss. In the next round, we faced Dunfermline at East End Park, but lost 7-0. Flavell's reaction was curt, 'Next time we play in the cup, you lot go to the bookies first!'

I was 33 years of age and, although I still enjoyed playing, my best days were behind me. At the end of the season Flavell said that he would like me to stay, but if I wanted to go he would respect my wishes. I decided the time had come to hang up my boots after a wonderful career. It was an easy decision to make because the wonderful memories I had under the great Bill Struth were cherished and I realised that I could never return to these halcyon days. In many ways my career had ended on a whimper, but no one could take away the fabulous times that I had enjoyed in my career, particularly at Ibrox. Fifteen years had passed since I first arrived in Scotland with no more than dreams and a lot of hope. Mr Struth had given me the opportunity to fulfil these dreams and things had now come full circle. My time as a player had ended and now I had to contemplate where my career and my life would take me. The time had come to open another chapter.

It is very difficult to leave football and my first instinct was to get back into the game as a manager. I had my coaching badges, of course, and I felt that I had a lot to offer the game. An opportunity came up at Dumbarton, which I applied for, but nothing came of it. There were no other opportunities that came up afterwards, as I began to realise that I would need to find something to do out of the game. I was not the only one dealing with a crisis of change. When we moved to Prestwick, we had some excitement that there was an opportunity in the shop with Ella too. However, she just hated it and so we decided that it was best to sell the house with the shop and move to another house in the town. In the past, every new change we had made revolved around my football. This time, the changes would be driven by the end of my career and Ella's desire to shake free from the shackles of the shop. We sold up and moved to a house in Pleasantfield Road, Prestwick. Now I would have to find a job.

15

The Community Servant

WHEN the curtain came down on my football career at 33, I had to come to terms with the reality that I would have to get back into regular work. I did not have a trade and my only work experience of any note had been in the sports shops in Glasgow and Pretoria. In the early stages of my career I had worked in an office and, of course, on the council's roads back home in South Africa. However, neither of these stints provided sufficient experience for me to seriously suggest that I could use them in a CV to back up an application for similar work. In reality, apart from working in shops, I did not seem to be suited to any particular job.

Fortunately, I had some friends at Prestwick Airport who were aware that I was keen to get into work. They asked around and managed to get me fixed up on the duty crew. The new terminal building had just opened and the airport was in a phase of expansion. After a short time working in and around the terminal, I was assigned to driving one of the Lister vehicles, which transported materials around the airport. It was very different from life as a footballer, of course, but it was welcome. Like everyone else, I needed an income and the work helped me get back into life away from the football ground.

I remained at the airport for two years, but I had a hankering to get back into sport in some capacity. Importantly, since I had completed my coaching certificates at the SFA, I was keen to apply what I learned. One day I decided to call the education authorities to see if there was perhaps an opportunity to coach some of the schoolkids, although I knew that I would be an uncertified teacher. They told me that they had a vacancy for a part-time PE teacher, which I could fulfil with my existing certificates. During my time at Rangers I had also learned to coach cricket, badminton and tennis, so I thought that I would have a lot to offer the kids, although the schools were most interested in my football coaching.

I was delighted to take up the position and was assigned to my first school – Ardrossan Academy. I remained there for a few months and then I was transferred to Kilmaurs Academy, before my final placement in St Michael's Academy in Kilwinning. The role I had in each was to give the youngsters some proper football coaching. I found that I had a good rapport with the kids and they were very attentive in my classes. The exception was one youngster at St Michaels. Unlike the two previous schools, which were non-denominational,

St Michael's was Roman Catholic. A lot of the children were Celtic fans and they knew that I was a former Rangers player, but I commanded their attention – except one young lad called Jimmy. I had been told about Jimmy before I took the class. Apparently he was disruptive and a bit of a troublemaker.

In my first class I gathered all of the kids around to explain what we were going to do. Jimmy remained about 20 yards away from the group, with no apparent interest in what was going on. At that I told the kids how we would get organised to play a game and to his great surprise, I shouted that Jimmy would show everyone what to do. He said that he did not know what to do and I told him quite forcibly that he *would* know what to do if he came and joined the group. At that, he came over to join us and I had his attention. From that point I worked on Jimmy to make sure that he was part of things and I never had any trouble with him.

A few years ago, Ella and I were in the Lake District when a car came alongside us at our hotel and tried to park up in a restricted area. I told the driver, who had a Scots accent, that he could not park there, but I showed him a couple of areas where he could park. He looked at me and I thought I recognised him. I asked him where he came from and at that he said, 'Mr Hubbard?' It turned out that he was at St Michael's School at that time and he recalled the situation with Jimmy. He told me that from that moment, when I pulled Jimmy into the group, he became a totally different character. Prior to that, nobody had liked Jimmy and he had isolated himself. Apparently, afterwards, from being the most disliked boy in the school, he became one of the most popular.

He had changed and the school had no more bother with him.

I do not know whatever happened to Jimmy and the chap I spoke with did not know either. However, I told him that if it had all worked out well with Jimmy, who was a keen Celtic fan, it was at least one good thing I had done for our Old Firm rivals!

During the school holidays, the summer months were quiet, so I managed to get a job at the local Butlins camp, as a Redcoat. I was mainly a supervisor over the part-time staff in the bars, but I did some coaching there too. It was another bit of experience, but I enjoyed the opportunity to work with the kids over a longer period, rather than just the duration of their holiday.

I remained with the education authorities for two years and, during this time, when I was not working at the weekends, I used to enjoy watching or playing cricket down at our local Prestwick club. One day, when I was watching the cricket along with a chap who turned out to be the Burgh Surveyor, I remarked that I could make good use of the four resurfaced tennis courts next to the cricket field. I had watched two young girls playing on the courts but the facility seemed underused. I thought that, with my experience in tennis, I could perhaps offer some assistance in revitalising the club. The courts always seemed to be empty, but otherwise provided a good tennis facility.

He liked the idea and suggested a meeting with the Lord Provost. He also thought it was a good idea and I started coaching lessons and soon formed a proper club. We put an advert in the local newspaper, offering coaching lessons and looking for new members. In that first week when I just got involved, they had four senior members and 11 junior members in the club. Within ten days, after the advert went in, we had 34 senior members and 68 junior members! The coaching classes became very popular and the council invested more and more into the facilities. The club became bigger and bigger and was highly respected in the sport nationally. We organised tennis tournaments that became very popular and they attracted some great players.

We always organised a tournament each year, for the week before Wimbledon and in 1977, a young girl from South Africa called Greer Stevens entered. She was due to play at the All England Club the following week and wanted to use our tournament as a warm-up. When she turned up at Prestwick, she had her father with her. As we got chatting, he asked my name and then told me that he had played football against me back in South Africa. He had played with Natal and we met when I was playing for Northern Transvaal. I cannot remember if he was any good at football, but his daughter was very good at tennis.

That year after competing at Prestwick, she went to Wimbledon and won the mixed doubles crown. She won again in 1979 and later that year won the mixed doubles at the US Open. That we had a player of such quality at our tournament gives some idea of the standing that we reached.

Following the success of the tennis club, I asked to be taken on full-time with the council, where I planned to use the winter to teach different schools and take the kids at night for different sports. I took them for football on Mondays and Thursdays, badminton on Saturday afternoon, gymnastics on Friday, with the help of a gymnast, and golf on the Friday, assisted by the local professional Frank Rennie. When the local authorities were regionalised in 1975, I was asked by the new council if I could do anything with an underused facility, Dam Park Hall in Ayr. I jumped at the chance. By then, as the community sports officer, I was looking after 400 kids every week at Prestwick, so the hall opened up the opportunity to make something happen there.

I had different sports organised every day and night, and managed to coerce some local help to create three football pitches. I then started a five-a-side tournament for kids at Christmas and then they became so frequent that several were held each year and I reckon that in the 30 years that the tournaments ran, over 250,000 kids took part, ranging in age from under the age of seven to 18. The tournaments were a huge success and a number of youngsters went on to become great players themselves, including Rangers' Barry Ferguson and Kris Boyd.

The tournaments ran for almost 20 years at Dam Park Hall but then they transferred to a new facility called Whitletts Shoot Super Soccer project, which created a number of five-a-side pitches. Around that time and feeling that I had put a lot into the community, I thought it was time to retire. However, they asked me to manage the operations at Whitletts, which I duly did, intending to give it only a couple more years. Seven years later I was still there until I finally retired at 66 in 1997, although I had not quite finished there. They asked me once again to help out with their autumn tournament and then run another at Christmas. I then started an under-11 side which I managed and coached, all the time maintaining my devotion to Rangers by acting as a scout for the club and coaching boys on Rangers' behalf in Whitletts.

During this time I never gave up on cricket and in 1984, I was elected captain of Prestwick Cricket Club. It was a sport I was always comfortable in and I was hitting regular centuries. However, I kept saying that this is my last season, but I could not seem to give up playing. Sport had been my life and if I was not coaching, I wanted to play. It is how it had always been.

After over 30 years of community service, I decided that at last, I should hang up my boots, bat, racket and leave the ball at the door. It meant that I could spend more time with my family, as well as providing an opportunity to visit Ibrox again on a more regular basis. It was then, in May 1998, that I received the ultimate accolade of an Honorary MBE in recognition of my services to football, as well as to the local community and in particular young people. I received the honour at a ceremony in Ayr's County Buildings by the Lord Lieutenant of Ayrshire and Arran Major Richard Henderson, with my family proudly in attendance. It was very humbling.

If this was not enough, I was then greatly honoured to have been elected into the Rangers Hall of Fame in 2008. Again, I found the presentation of the award and the induction of my name to join so many Rangers greats to be quite overwhelming.

Today, as I look back over my career and my life, I realise how fortunate I have been. From my wonderful early life in South Africa I found a new home in Scotland that was to continue the happiness I had enjoyed in my formative years with mom, my brother, sisters and not forgetting Martha. In Glasgow, I found the love of my life, Ella and we shared lovely children in Linda, Raymond and John, who gave us our eight beautiful grandchildren. If the great umpire in the sky had allowed me to plan out my life any better, I could not have done so.

I have met some wonderful friends along the way and played with some great clubs, but among them all is the one I consider the greatest – Rangers Football Club. It was there that my career was guided by one of the legends of the game – Bill Struth. And through all of this has been the immense support I have had from fans of every colour. It was a great pleasure playing for each and every one of you and I hope you have enjoyed this little journey through my life.

Reflections

by Craig Brown CBE, former Scotland international team manager

I HAVE nothing but fond memories of the times I spent with Johnny Hubbard, both during my playing days and also when I moved into coaching. I started off my professional football career with Rangers and, although I did not break through to the first team, I had the pleasure of being at Ibrox for a short time near the end of Johnny's career. My great memory of Johnny is that he was great for all of the young players at the club, always offering support and encouragement. At that time everyone trained together, reserves and first team players alike, so it was always important to the youngsters to have respect for, and from, the older players. As one of the youngsters, I can say that we looked up to Johnny and he was always a man we could turn to for advice. He was also great to have around the dressing room. But there was one occasion, some time later, when I was delighted to have him around for quite different reasons. He saved me £50!

In 1973, a few years after we had both left the club, Rangers celebrated their centenary with a match against Arsenal at Ibrox. The club's general manager was former player Willie Waddell and he invited several of the past players to join in the celebrations. I had never played a competitive match for the first team, so I wrote to Waddell and told him that I appreciated his kind invitation, but that I would be embarrassed to turn up as a player alongside all of these great Rangers legends. He wrote to me saying that he regarded every player to be part of the club's history and that I would be rightfully there.

I knew Johnny well and quite separately, he asked me if I was going. I told him of my dilemma but Johnny told me that I had to go, because he needed a lift from Prestwick! I lived in the area then and since Hubbie didn't drive at the time, I often picked him up.

Anyway, we headed off to Ibrox that night and as we neared the ground a little late, we searched around for a parking place. It was a big crowd, so we struggled to find anywhere near to the stadium. As we were driving along Dumbreck Road, a policeman directed us to park herring-bone into the kerb, as they tried to relieve the congestion. I parked up and then we headed off to the ground. At the end of the game, we joined the rest of the official party at the Rangers Social Club before making our way back to the car. When we arrived at the place where the car had been, there was no sign of it. I flagged down a police car, thinking it had been stolen, to be told it had been taken to the police pound at Pollokshields. Apparently it was considered to be illegally parked. They gave us a lift as the rain began to fall. Johnny, with bunnet pulled over his forehead, and I walked into the station to recover my car.

I told the big officer that we had been told to park there, but he was having none of it and told me that there was a £50 fine to get it released. I gave him my name as it would be in the registration certificate – James Craig Brown, and told him that we had been guests of Rangers as former players.

He said, 'What the f*** are you talking about? I've been a Rangers fan all my life and I've never heard of a former player called "James Craig Brown". Pay up the £50 and get your a**** out of here the two of you.' But I pleaded, 'He played for Rangers too', pointing to Hubbie. 'This is Johnny Hubbard,' I said as Johnny lifted his bunnet slowly. The startled officer looked at the wee man in awe, then rushed around the desk to give him a big hug. 'Johnny Hubbard – Johnny Hubbard! What a great honour to meet you Johnny – I was a big fan of yours. Johnny Hubbard, what a man!' Needless to say, he ripped up the charge and we drove out of the station and back down to Ayrshire, with my £50 still intact!

Back in 1989, when I was the coach of the Scotland Under-16 team, we reached the final of the World Cup only for the boys to lose out to Saudi Arabia 5-4 on penalties. After the disappointment had subsided, I called Johnny to ask him if he would come to Largs to give a coaching session to the players. With Johnny's expertise from the penalty spot, I thought it would be a great opportunity for the youngsters as well as the SFA coaches to draw on his experience and ability. It worked very well and we videotaped the session. I gather from Johnny that even some time later, players and goalkeepers who benefitted from his tips and coaching would often call on him to thank him for his tips.

It was not all serious stuff, however, and I can remember once when he had us in stitches. There were lots of famous faces gathered around Johnny as he told them of his technique in taking penalties. They listened attentively as we stood on the pitch then, after explaining how he approached the spot-kick, he said he would show us the different styles used by other players who were equally famed for their penalties. He said that he would show them a 'David Lapsley penalty', then asked the players to clear the edge of the penalty area while he took his run-up.

Lapsley, who had appeared in the St Mirren team that won the Scottish Cup in 1959, was famed for his long run-up to the ball when he took a penalty. As the players cleared the area and the goalkeeper stood on the line, Johnny slowly trudged back from the ball, walking further and further until he reached the halfway line. He then started his run and as he reached the penalty box, he slowed, puffing and panting, before stopping just before he reached the ball. Then he toe-ended it past the keeper.

The players were in uproar, but little did they know that it was a pretty good impression of how Lapsley did actually approach his penalties! Hubbie had them in the palm of his hand and they learned a lot that day from our little session – indeed it was a masterclass.

As I said, I have many fine memories of Johnny, both on and off the field and it has been my enormous pleasure to know him and contribute in this small way to his book. He is a remarkable man and there is no doubt that his contribution to Rangers and the game in Scotland has been immense.

Johnny Hubbard – Rangers Career Details

Debut: 10 September 1949 (Rangers 2 Partick Thistle 0 – Scottish First Division, at Ibrox Stadium. Attendance 60,000)

Final Match: 29 November 1958 (Motherwell 2 Rangers 2 – Scottish First Division, at Fir Park. Attendance 32,977)

Honours: Championships: 3 – (1952/53, 1955/56, 1956/57)

Scottish Cup 1 – (1952/53)

International Caps: 1 (v Scotland)

	Appearances	Goals
Scottish First Division	172	75
Scottish League Cup	41	22
Scottish Cup	19	5
Europe	6	1
Competitive Total	238	103
Other Matches	62	26
Overall Total	300	129

Competitive Appearances by Season

Season	League	League Cup	Scottish Cup	Europe	TOTAL
1949/50	2	-	-	-	2
1950/51	8(2)	-	-	-	8(2)
1951/52	1	-	-	-	1
1952/53	24	1	7(2)	-	32(2)
1953/54	15	9(1)	1	-	25(1)
1954/55	23(13)	3(1)	3	-	29(14)
1955/56	34(17)	9(10)	3	-	46(27)
1956/57	33(15)	6(4)	3(2)	3(1)	45(22)
1957/58	24(19)	7(2)	2(1)	3	36(22)
1958/59	8(9)	6(4)	-	-	14(13)

Johnny Hubbard's penalty statistics in official matches during his time with Rangers.

Date	Opponents	Venue	Time (mins)	
24 May 1954	British Columbia	A	?	
28 August 1954	Stirling Albion	H	87	
16 October 1954	Partick Thistle	A	58	
23 October 1954	Dundee	H	78	
30 October 1954	St Mirren	A	43	
06 November 1954	Kilmarnock	H	71	
27 November 1954	Raith Rovers	H	26	
01 January 1955	Celtic	H	89	
26 March 1955	Queen of the South	H	85	
11 April 1955	Partick Thistle	H	60	
19 May 1955	Racing Paris	A	?	
17 August 1955	Falkirk	H	42	
07 September 1955	Irish League	H	21	
08 October 1955	Airdrie	H	83	
26 November 1955	Motherwell	H	10	
17 December 1955	Hibernian	H	65	
26 December 1955	Celtic	A	43	
07 January 1956	Dundee	H	4	
21 January 1956	East Fife	H	58	
28 January 1956	Airdrie	A	75	Missed
12 March 1956	Scotland	A	?	
17 March 1956	Hearts	A	70	
24 March 1956	Kilmarnock	A	39	
07 April 1956	Raith Rovers	A	48	
11 August 1956	East Fife	H	74	
25 August 1956	East Fife	A	81	
01 September 1956	Aberdeen	H	61	
17 September 1956	Partick Thistle	H	62	
29 September 1956	Ayr United	H	24	
10 October 1956	Clyde	H	71	
13 October 1956	Partick Thistle	H	67	
03 November 1956	Hibernian	H	65	
14 November 1956	Nice	A	40	
24 November 1956	Aberdeen	H	30	
22 December 1956	Kilmarnock	A	27	Missed
02 February 1957	Hearts	A	26	
16 February 1957	Celtic	A	83	
23 February 1957	Queens Park	H	69	
16 March 1957	Falkirk	H	?	Missed
27 April 1957	Queen of the South	A	15	
31 August 1957	Raith Rovers	A	26	
07 September 1957	Queen of the South	H	80	
14 September 1957	Kilmarnock	H	23	
02 November 1957	Queens Park	A	68	
09 November 1957	Kilmarnock	H	54	
23 November 1957	Falkirk	A	42	
	Falkirk	A	89	
14 December 1957	Dundee	A	59	
22 February 1958	Queens Park	H	60	
10 March 1958	Kilmarnock	A	27	
	Kilmarnock	A	62	
12 April 1958	Third Lanark	A	17	
	Third Lanark	A	60	
03 May 1958	Airdrie	H	23	
13 August 1958	Raith Rovers	A	64	
23 August 1958	Hearts	A	47	
27 August 1958	Raith Rovers	H	88	
01 September 1958	Third Lanark	A	79	
06 September 1958	Celtic	A	41	
13 September 1958	Partick Thistle	H	29	
20 September 1958	Airdrie	A	54	
04 October 1958	Dunfermline	A	71	
25 November 1958	Grasshoppers	H	78	

The statistics does not include goals scored in unofficial matches, including those scored in matches played with the RAF, the details of which were unavailable.